Dancing with God:
A Theology of Joy

Dr. James McReynolds

Parson's Porch Books

Dancing with God: A Theology of Joy
ISBN: Softcover 978-1540460004
Copyright © 2016 by James McReynolds

To order additional copies of this book, contact:

Parson's Porch Books
1-423-475-7308
www.parsonsporch.com

Parson's Porch Books is an imprint of Parson's Porch & Company (PP&C) in Cleveland, Tennessee. PP&C is an innovative company which raises money by publishing books of noted authors, representing all genres. All donations from contributors and profits from publishing are shared with the poor.

Dancing with God:
A Theology of Joy

Contents

Acknowledgments 7

Dedication 9

Foreword by John Killinger 11

Introduction 15

Chapter One
Cultivating Joy in the People of God 21

Chapter Two
Joy as a Transformation Movement 25

Chapter Three
Dancing with God Through Depression 29

Chapter Four
Living the Good Life with Joy 33

Chapter Five
Ministries of Joy to the World's Need
for Love and Compassion 37

Chapter Six
Joylessness of All Generations in Dying Churches 41

Chapter Seven
Music for the Dance with God   45

Chapter Eight
Searchlights and Flashlights: Happiness and Joy   51

Chapter Nine
Jesus Came to Bring Joy and Happiness to a   57
World Starved for Love

Chapter Ten
Journeys with Joy and Strength in the Lord   63

Chapter Eleven
Joy at the Beginning and End of the Cosmic Dance   70

Chapter Twelve
Discovering Joy in Scripture   76

Chapter Thirteen
When the Dancing Stops   81

Chapter Fourteen
Will You Join in the New Dance?   89

Chapter Fifteen
Dancing Gracefully Together   96

Author's Biography   103

Acknowledgments

Writing books and articles is a gift of my ministry. Many of my insights about a theology of joy come out of preaching, coaching, and 65 years of reflecting on joy. I have attempted to convey faithfully the essence of what the emotion joy is. The congregations, the students, those in prisons, nursing homes, small support groups, and hospitals with whom I have shared my joy as I listened to their joys helped in developing this book. John Killinger has contributed to every phase of my work since my days as a student at Vanderbilt University Divinity School. John's wisdom is woven within these pages. A host of librarians have pointed me to resources.

My village includes readers throughout the world who pored over my words, concepts, and debatable theology. This book is "a" theology of joy, not, "the" theology of joy.

Matthew Fox's book, *Sheer Joy*, a massive and creative conversation with Thomas Aquinas was among the many books I read. Many I disagreed with as most still held the thought that joy is some unattainable experience that is not a onetime emotional experience, but is reflected in those who are unrealistically positive always and whose worship and life is always. rejoicing.

Thanks to the publishing team of Parson's Porch Books in Cleveland, Tennessee. I am so grateful to all of you that I could set music to my thankfulness in Carnegie Hall and do a dance on "Dancing with the Stars."

Dedication

When people have a positive attitude, they reflect a magnetic field of joyous energy around them. You can feel their happiness touch you from across a room. This field of joy is so magnetic; it attracts everyone and everything to them. The more positive you are, the happier you become, drawing likeminded people into your life. Joy is that powerful. "The joy of the Lord" creates a living drama for you to dance with God and experience joy and miracles. To my wife Laurel who has shared my struggles and my joys, and loved me unconditionally. To my daughter Linda and to Bryan, Carmen, and Carrie, step children who became my own. To their spouses whose global military service enabled many adventures of grace, love, and joy. To my mentor Dr. John Killinger who has believed in me and encouraged me to help make my ministry a reality. To my two brothers, Ed and David McReynolds; to my colleagues and Friends in the Christian Church (Disciples of Christ) and the ecumenical kingdom of God where I have served on local church staffs in 12 denominations: friends from throughout the world with whom I have shared my theology of joy.

May your souls eternally enjoy the infinite beauty and joys of heaven.

Foreword

We all live in a world of pain and suffering—of wars, poverty, disease, mental instability, moral impurity, aging, and death. Our daily news reports are crammed with negative messages and images. Many of us feel inundated by problems and reasons to be unhappy.

What could be more important, in such a world, than James McReynolds' message about joy and love?

This isn't a new message from Jim. He's been beating this drum for many years now. He has had his own problems. I remember a night when I was away from home on a speaking trip. Jim phoned our house in the middle of the night. My wife Anne answered the call and heard his desperate voice on the other end, threatening to end his life. She talked to him until dawn, and then sent a friend of his to his house to make sure he was all right.

Then Jim discovered the concept of joy. He tells about it in this book. It changed his life. He has been an evangelist for joy ever since, flying all over the country and even the world to tell people how important it is.

How many of us experience real joy on a regular basis? Not many, I'm sure.

I had my own brush with depression a few years ago. I had gone from being a professor in an elite university to being the pastor of a busy church. I was working my fanny off being an administrator, a counselor, a preacher, and all the other things a pastor must be. And it wasn't long before I began to feel blah and think maybe I'd made a bad move.

There was a young lady psychologist who had come to me for help with some of her patients' problems, so one day I told her she owed me some free counseling and started complaining about my depression. After listening to me for a few minutes, she said, "I'm giving you an assignment. Next week, when we talk again, I want you to show me the lists you have made of the small joys in your daily life." I started keeping a list. Usually there were ten or fifteen things I might not have noticed as joys if I hadn't been looking for them. Small things. Little bursts of pleasure. I ran across these lists only recently. There were such things on them as "Watched a bee sucking nectar from a flower," "Felt the dew on my ankle as I walked through the grass to fetch the morning paper," "Enjoyed the taste of a good jambalaya," "Admired the overspreading of stars in the night sky," and "Loved the feeling of my wife's chin nuzzling against my neck as I left for work."

Within six weeks, I was a new man. My depression was gone, and I was thrilled by the sensations of my common, everyday life. I continued to make the lists for a long time because it was always a pleasure to think back on each day's sensations and write down the things that had moved my heart and emotions.

So, I know the importance of James McReynolds' work. If more people noticed all the joys that surround them every day, exploding like fireworks in their dark and glorious skies, there would be fewer wars, fewer crimes, and more sheer excitement about being alive.

This book bristles with Jim's thoughts about the joyful life. He talks about it on every page. No one can read the book without coming away thinking about joy and what it means to his or her life. I wish it were required reading for everybody, regardless of age or stage of life. There would be an immediate and noticeable leap in the world's wellness quotient!

John Killinger

Introduction

The Westminster Confession of Faith has been a foundation for Christian theology.

I have studied joy for more than 50 years. I was introduced to joy in a doctor of ministry class at Vanderbilt University Divinity School. The course was taught by Chris Meadows, who earned his Ph.D. at Princeton with a dissertation on joy.

During the first day of class, words from the Westminster Confession of Faith were spoken. In considering a theology of joy, those words, "the chief and highest end is to glorify God and enjoy (God) forever" ring true.

Quickly Dr. Meadows and the class discussion revealed how difficult it would be to define joy or to understand what it means "to glorify God and enjoy him forever." Vanderbilt put this class in their clergy training curriculum because the Church and society need a way to articulate the theology that will bring health and salvation to the world in unity with God and in community with one another to fulfill the destiny of humans everywhere. That has been the focus of my ministry. Twenty years after I spent years preaching a theology of joy, I was attending Dr. Norman Vincent Peale's School of Practical Christianity. Peale expressed excitement and agreement that joy was a vital topic like his own power of positive thinking. Peale as only Peale can do, said, "I anoint you as the minister of joy to the world."

So, I preached, taught, and wrote with "joy" as the key to understanding and living in the Kingdom of God. During recent years, the Templeton Foundation awarded Yale University Divinity School a multi-million-dollar grant for scholars to study "joy." I offered to contribute as the project directors said that no one had ever studied joy.

I said, "I beg to differ, but I have written 12 books and thousands of sermons with the theme 'joy.'" I mailed my published works to Yale, but I never heard from them. I traveled to New Haven several times and the school allowed me and others to attend some lectures and to enjoy their excellent library.

I write for God's pleasure. Agnes Hull, my English professor at Carson-Newman University told me that I had "a gift, a poetic soul." I recently re-read *Sheer Joy*, the creative 532-page book by Matthew Fox which was written as a long interview on theology and spirituality with conversations with Thomas Aquinas. Dr. Morris Ashcraft, my theology teacher at Midwestern Baptist Seminary, said theology was vital in helping churches fulfill their mission and for us not to get sucked in to a false and unhealthy understanding of who God is. In my vision "to create an atmosphere where joy and miracles happen," I have experienced multitudes of people find happiness and sheer joy in their lives. In previous books, I have expressed what I mean by joy. My teaching, preaching, writing, counseling, and coaching have had the goal of transforming the Church and God's children into a movement centered on joy, and what Christians and non-believers agree or disagree on what joy is.

A healthy theology of joy cultivates our fitness for heaven. It is the reception of our gifts for here and now. Thanking and praising God for our gifts is the ultimate telos of joy. Preaching and teaching lead people to receive the gifts of joy today. In the Scriptures, joy is a fruit of the Spirit. The positive psychology movement has helped in understanding the power of joy as beyond imagination.

Paul writes, quoting Isaiah 64:4, "eye has not seen, nor ear heard, neither has the heart conceived, the things that God has prepared for those who love (God)" in I Corinthians 2:9.

In moments of our living, people are "in a joy" but not comprehending, but placing that memory on videos in our mind to be retrieved later. Any reflection amplifies the theology of joy as the sight of your child being born. Joy is not a general mood. Perhaps happiness is along with other emotions such as anger, anxiety, fear, and guilt being part of our days of living. Harold Bales, a colleague in the class on joy at Vanderbilt said that joy is a responsive act of exaltation and gratitude. When Paul writes "to rejoice always," I think he's communicating not about the human emotion joy, but happiness as a positive view of life itself.

If I were ever to start another congregation, I would call the Spirit of Joy Christian Church. This fits my theology of joy and church. Church is to create an atmosphere or environment in which people inside or in the outside community will create structure to help cultivate joy as individuals become fit citizens of the kingdom of heaven now. Grace comes from our times of joy. Every job, every experience, every gift has come always as a surprise. A healthy theology of joy provides a thoughtful framework within which to understand Church communications as the means for enabling people to hold on to a deliberative life that cultivates joy. Theology is the attempt to dance with God, to catch the rhythm is a way of dancing. God always takes the lead. Will Christians today support a church that is centered on joy? If a church's focus is on joy alone, critics will say that joy might be risking the absence of justice or traditional worship.

The word "joy" is used to sell everything from washing powder, automobiles, social events, and all that comes with our current consumerist mindset. Joy is admittedly not the whole purpose of our goals. And so, joy becomes a human term applied to spiritual realities.

Christians need not fall into the traps of worldly pleasures acting in place of spiritualties of joy. So, joy becomes the least discussed human emotion in most divinity schools or churches. And, among psychiatrists, scholars, and those who refuse to change their perceptions. So, Christians must proceed with caution, however, a healthy theology of joy will produce new visions and more effective living. Thinking theologically about this positive experience and finding the purpose for our churches will help stop the bleeding among the mainline denominations that are dying every day. More than 1,000 local congregations close their doors every day.

A circumspective theology of joy will help people name and comprehend the challenges that faces those who realize that there are snakes in our world's gardens today. Much of our teaching that results in a theology of joy is intra-Christian. Some call it discipleship. Christians must care about the social conditions within the steeples of our buildings. If churches are to continue to exist, they must work within their communities. Fortunately, the concept of joy has an appeal far from spiritual communities. People also care about joy who have never, as the saying goes, "darkened the door of a church." I used the same basic concepts when I served as a psychiatric therapist at the Lincoln Regional Center where we worked to improve the lives of those hardened by serious mental disorders and heinous crimes against humanity. Even the few billionaires living with little concerns are desperately seeking "fullness" in life. Sheer joy involves specific visions which motivate most individuals and communities in our planet today.

An honest theology of joy will aid us with those who are not Christian. And it should help us in inter-religious communications. As we travel to distant nations, we can coach, counsel, and just talk with those of no religion. This movement of joy will be vital in coming decades. The concept of joy will more and more shape various people. The experience of joy has grown more difficult to understand as limited life and planet rush on in utter joylessness. There are tensions between positive psychologists and theologians and strictly secular views that are common today. Most secularists do not see any reason for having a concept of joy. Yet the desire in each soul is to build a wealth of joy in a world starved for love.

Chapter One
Cultivating Joy in The People of God

A healthy theology is the one essential in living our destiny as humans in relationship with God. Theology enables communities of faith to communicate an understanding of faith.

That is what the creeds, statements of faith, disciplines, and other attempts to enable people to know God "and enjoy Him forever," is about.

So, this book is another strategic spiritual journey to enable healthy transformation in our communities and families and what that means. Part of the problems—losing young adults and youth and children and even the multitude of older adults who lack the passion and attraction can discover a healthy theology of joy in juxtaposition to secular culture with whom Christians can find common cause in the human struggle to cultivate an environment where joy can happen.

Becoming aware of ourselves through prayer, coaching, counseling, and psychotherapy is a key to cultivation of times of joy.

Joy is provoked by something that is mostly outside ourselves. Every hug from a child, a time of realizing the uniqueness of the universe, the birth of a child, the graduation ceremony as the diploma or an ordination certificate is placed in the hand. Joy is an intimate time in oneself that strengthens ego and esteem. We could say that a joy experience is sacramental.

The Kingdom of God is within us. It is Good News of "great joy." The Great Commission is to act (go into all the world) to help cultivate an atmosphere for joy, which is the church's ultimate purpose. If a body of Christ does not live in grace and in times of sheer joy, it will gravitate to fear, guilt, anger, anxiety, the dominant emotions of a dying church.

Worship will yield to cultivating the pleasures in current culture. Preaching and teaching a theology of God will result in individuals learning and centering on the story of God and God's saving action.

That kind of cultivation creates a communal and personal response to those stories. That is our new strategic journey to a theology of joy. Church is not static, but moves with action as the body is trained to invite the Holy Spirit to practice becoming the love of God. Each Christian will be aware that each is on the way in this training. Soul healing is not something humans do, but what is done by God's guidance by the Spirit.

The theology of joy is evangelical. The current church disregards the terms evangelical and evangelism. The joy movement is not a completely new thing. From the beginning the goal of soul healing brings a deeper and wider communion with God. A theology of joy enables people to understand the Holy Spirit, to catch his rhythm and to dance with God. God takes the lead. Theology of joy is not reaching to meet the demands for church relevance or success. Joy exists at the junction of transcendence and immanence. Joyful living is not a problem to be solved, but a mystery to be lived.

Joy is just one dimension of the fruit of the Spirit. I would never say that the church should focus on just joy alone. We must go deep not shallow as some erroneous understanding of joy could cause the church to return to a consumerist mindset. Most humans believe the lies of society equating joy with pleasure, prosperity, and selfish indulgence.

A healthy theology of joy explains divine realties. In one of my churches where I served as pastor, we started articulating a theology of joy with 100 days of prayer. Only then could we focus on the fruit of the Spirit and the most misunderstood human emotion. That is the root of the challenger to share "the joy of the Lord" as the strength of our faith and our work. All Christians are ministers. I have published 13 books on joy. I write for God's pleasure. Never in history has the Christian life been so full of new challenges. As an active retired ordained minister, in my last stage of life, I know I'll not be asked to teach or preach as much as in the past. So, I want to help churches minister to older adults and find a way to help older people to find fruitful ministry. In our time, 1,000 people celebrate their 70th birthday every single day. The human capacity for joy is under attack.

In our society dissatisfaction is cultivated in the products we buy and the products themselves. I lost the first pages of this book to scammers who invaded my life, stole my computer stored stuff. We must buy a new computer most every two years. We cannot be content with any of them. Most of us just think, "Well, that's the reality of life." And so just a few people with money and control make life's environment create a negative, joyless life. Even non-believers want to find joy. That might be a harbinger of the importance of spreading our theology of joy. This movement toward wholeness is aimed toward healing.

Chapter Two

Joy as a Transformation Movement

Many denominated or even non-denominational communities of faith call themselves "movements." Many movements are unhealthy. Their goals are to control and to keep people in ignorance, in depression, in shame, in alienation and isolation, in exclusion, in frustration, even in violence and misery.

Some movements involve the sense of potential. These see beyond our assumptions. They help us reframe our thinking toward possibilities that go beyond our current sufferings and constraints.

Movements arise in situations characterized by the thwarting or denial of joy. We see this in the Reformation, the Wesleyan resistance in the Anglican church, the Anabaptists and the Baptist formations, the Campbell's and the Christian churches, and a thousand movements throughout history.

In our theology of joy, we cannot be involved in the emotional energy created in peak experiences of big mobilizations. What we call flow does not continue. We always must go back to our daily living with mundane chores, obligations, distractions, pressures, and fragmentations.

Just how do we incorporate continuing joy into our lives? My mentor Dr. John Killinger shared a random thought.

He wrote, "Every mountaintop experience is a great joy. Every joy ought to be a mountaintop experience."

And the very nature of this experience involves going back down into the valley. There we confront barriers due to institutionalized power arrangements and the cultures of exclusion and violence. So, we must deal with these challenges in our communities, our families, and the workplace arena. In these contexts, we must communicate and disseminate joy.

Losing track of a theology of joy has happened in many generations. A part of this is in our visioning and imagining dancing during a joyful congregation, aroused by the Good News bringing blessings and delight.

Joy is the emotion that stirs arousal. Multitudes, including youth who have no realistic concept of the dimensions of passion, delude themselves by thinking," If it feels good, it must be God." Joy awakens them and they feel fully alive. Joy fits our dream of not being contained or restrained.

Human desire for arousal is not just our biology, especially youth. Teens long to know passion. They long to be loved and to love to the point of suffering. When the world's market leaders sell sex to the adolescents, they address their need for arousal.

The media's portrayal of sex feels more joyful than the church's foundation of faith. Faith or theology means nothing to most teens. A few are highly devoted. Their arousal to life is a sacred awakening.

Arousal stimulates youthful desire for other or another. Joy is an exuberance which in Latin means "abundantly fruitful." Joy is a seed of life. How many times have youth returned from summer church camp with tales of finding the love of their life? Spiritual highs and camp romances are youth ministry realities that counselors must be connected. The experience of joy begets more joy. Joy moves beyond itself.

Dr. John Killinger said, "Every joy is preparation for the next one." Of course, joy is sometimes erotic. The Greek word *eros* is used for the love that is soul ecstasy.

A joy time moves us closer to others and we are beside ourselves. We cannot wait to share a joy with others. We jump, shout, act differently. The criterion for excellence with younger people is, "Did it move me?" If a concert with loud alluring music and sexy looking singers bring arousal. .and the church does not, the concert always wins.

Most younger people are constantly on the go. To get "high" or to" take a trip" too often means using drugs. Youth are swept off their feet by romance. Youth lose themselves in sports, music, and dancing. They get a buzz from driving risky or fast in their cars. They challenge themselves by jumping into water, or through watching lighting fast paced movies.

Another Killinger thought: "When I get to the point where I don't enjoy my life, it is time for me to die into another world of joy." That is the essence of what not only youth bur people of all ages and generations are now thinking. Suicides rates are high among teens, young people returning from war, and older people being left alone, and missing all the joys that happen in the final third of life.

The circle of life means to honor every day of our lives. Our years can be filled with a spirituality and theology of joy reflected in the words of the French philosopher Albert Camus: "In the midst of winter, I found in me an invincible summer." That invincible summer is in every one of us.

Chapter Three
Dancing with God Through Depression

Reinhold Niebuhr wrote a prayer that has guided millions. "God, Grant me serenity to accept the things I cannot change; courage to change the things I can, and the wisdom to know the difference. Living one day at a time; enjoying one moment at a time; accepting hardships as the pathway to peace: taking as He did, this sinful world as it is; not as I would have it: trusting that He will make all things right if I surrender to His will; that I may be reasonably happy in this life and supremely happy with Him forever in the next." Meister Eckhart wrote: "Truly it is in darkness that one finds the light, so when we are in sorrow, then the light is nearest of all to us."

Spirituality, a life lived in relationship with the Higher Power, has been found to be the most protective factor against depression known by medical practitioners.

The years of adolescence bring on depression. Many times, depression comes during the college years. These young people may continue to function, but still feel empty and unsure that life has purpose. Signs may include breaking up with a sweetheart of several years, staying in bed and missing class, and frustration. The successful outcome may not be learning to function better. It may be joy. During one period of my ministry, I served as a psychiatric therapist at a regional center, which was what we used to call a state hospital. I focused my group and individual therapy on the joy that is inside all seriously mentally ill patients. I used cognitive therapy and coaching questions that led some to see the ultimate presence of a Higher Power. Some begin to realize the blessings of daily life. Most therapists never understand that depression can be a way toward spiritual awakening.

Life sucking decisions, disastrous risk taking, and drug abuse cause joylessness. Discovering the positive, personal spirituality in people of all ages is the most healing factor for depression. We would be wrong to suggest that people with an understanding of joy have not continued to suffer. Resistance creates persistence in depression. Once a person achieves a strong spirituality within an environment of warmth, love, and forgiveness, she or he rarely suffers reoccurrence. Some mental health practitioners now understand depression as an opportunity to know happiness with all of life despite the negative emotions— fear, guilt, anger, anxiety—the seeds of joylessness. Some are diagnosed as having an adult adjustment disorder. There is still a stigma for those suffering from depression and other mental health problems. Youth with a personal relationship with God. These youths live in an environment where a theology of joy brings meaning and purpose and awareness of presence. This spiritual awakening could be called the Higher Power, the Great Spirit,

Hashem, Allah, or any word that brings on worship and a life filled with what we call the fruit of the Spirit. Every youth has sad days. Adolescents struggle with many negative people and experiences. Each event does not bring clinical depression. Ordinary struggles do not always lead to joylessness. Most therapists cannot understand depression as a spiritual problem. The Alcoholic Anonymous movement clearly is the most powerful spiritual movement that has proven that the way out of illness involves spirituality.

A spiritual vision quest toward joy is foundational for youth. Joy is not the result of using medications such as Prozac. It is critically important to deeply know that Joy, Love, God need our attention as we offer support for spiritual development.

In more than 40 years of speaking to youth in camps, in Youth for Christ, the Fellowship of Christian Athletes, and serving as a campus minister, I hear the cry of a spiritual emergence. I delivered my first baccalaureate address in 1966 at Hallsville High School in Hallsville, Missouri. That was in a different age in culture. God has used me to inspire youth in more than 100 high schools for this time of change and searching. Augustine's observance that "our hearts are restless until they find rest in Thee" declares we must have a felt and personal relationship with a Higher Power. Jesus said," The Kingdom of God is within you."

Authentic spiritual connection surges within us all, especially in the days of youth. Tyler Blevins who served as our youth minister at the First Christian Church in Weeping Water, Nebraska said a prayer before each wrestling match as he marched to win the state championship. He said he never prayed to win. He prayed to do his best. Every human being who has lived has their own vision quest for joy. The goal of each quest is for wholeness. Life is a spiritual journey full of struggle and pain. The joy movement requires us to meet every human where they are. The church must meet people in their community. Small groups dealing with mental illness, depression, abuse, anger, guilt and grief are invited into the building to find guidance and direction, and yes, a theology of God.

Keep on dancing with God and let your joy be unconfined.

Chapter Four
Living the Good Life with Joy

Building a model for the theology of joy is something that has been ignored by the church, by science, and by those reflecting on the good life.

Joy is a human emotion. In our lives, we know mostly negative emotions such as guilt, anger, anxiety, and fear. Nobody comes to a therapist or coach because they have too much joy in their lives. All emotions have an object. When we are afraid, we are afraid of something. If we feel guilt we have done something wrong or against cultural morals. If we are anxious, there is something causing the anxiety. If we are angry there is a reason or event that we have no control over. Human emotions reflect a person's interpretation of reality. Other life experiences such as lust, grief, sensations, and ecstasy involve emotions but are not emotions. Depending how deep one's concern about anything having an effect that is personal, the emotions expressed will vary in intensity. Intense anger may lead to murder.

And so, joy has an object such as the moment of new birth, the moment of surprise in receiving an award, scoring a winning touchdown or a last second successful shot in a basketball game.

When Saint Paul writes about "rejoicing," the word is more like happiness. Happiness is a searchlight of life with negative and positive emotions involved in the Good Life.

When we experience the emotion joy, it also varies in intensity. A child receiving a Christmas gift may jump up and down, shed tears, hug the parents, and say, "That's just what I wanted." An adult will feel joy that appears weak with a slight smile. Children used to sing the old chorus, "I have joy, joy, joy down in my heart to stay." Joy is remembered and placed in the videos of our brains to bring out later when times are difficult. No person can make themselves experience joy. Joy is a gift.

Joy comes as a surprise. Our will for joy is fulfillment of a natural desire. Pursuing joy is futile and self-defeating. Joy is not a possession to be grasped or bought. Things may be satisfying for those who feel entitled to all that comes into their living pathways. In a joy, we are most aware of the goodness and love of God. As joy is received, there is a harbinger of hope not only in this life, but in God's eternal life. When we die with happiness, we can say about Heaven. "I have just come from there." When we are surprised by joy, we know the Good Life. We accept God's gift with thanksgiving. We exist with confidence that our Father has showered us with love. We live in anticipation of renewed life coming despite our bodies growing old and weak. We are "going on to perfection" as the United Methodists proclaim. Perfect love is unconditional. Our joy in Heaven, however we might understand or imagine it, comes to those who are imperfect. Negative emotions will not exist in Heaven. Joy will. Every joy is preparation for the next one.

Our earthy journey is quite short. God's created children will make many missteps as we learn to dance with God. Abundant life is a never-ending dance of receiving and giving for the other person's journey.

If love and gifts of surprising joy are not flowing out of you, you are the one that does not allow God's gifts to flow toward you. Love flows toward us on earth as it will in heaven.

The Kingdom of God is already here—within us. Joy is an inner aliveness. Joy is not determined by an object enjoyed but by the prepared eyes of the enjoyer. In Baylor University's Armstrong-Browning Library, we read the words of Elizabeth Barrett Browning, "Earth's crammed with heaven, and every common bush afire with God." That's how good God is. Behind every mistaken description of the theology of God leads to a distorted image of God. Only God in you can know God and the nature of God's kingdom. We need in us "the mind of Christ."

None of us have God in our pocket. God knew us before we were born. God knows everything about us. He knows our eternal shape and our deepest identity. Scripture tells us that "our very hairs are numbered."

A theology of joy cannot be completely explained by human words. We may try using metaphors, analogies, similes, pictures to describe in approximation what joy means. If a person is both honest and humble, that child of God sees life as a mystery, not a problem that will ever be solved. If we try to use our religions to aggrandize the self, we will end up both proud and dishonest. If we do not approach God in humility and with honesty, our churches and religious communities worship themselves and their human formulations instead of God. God is not just a dancer. God is the dance itself. God our Creator invites us to participate in the divine dance which involves being loved and being loving.

Most of us came along on our earthly trip several years ago. We will be gone from this planet in just a few more years. The coming fully realized kingdom will not be designed for proud and power hungry people. Meaning is discovered not created. I pray you can say," I love you. I appreciate all you are and have been. Forgive me for any joylessness I might have enabled you to experience." In the end, the personal and family dynamics are the same. We live in fear or love, guilt or love, anxious or loving, in anger or love. Healthy communities are all about love. My mentor and longtime friend John Killinger wrote, "When I get to the point that I don't enjoy my life, it is time for me to die into another world of joy."

Chapter Five
Ministries of Joy to the World's Need for Love and Compassion

Theology is sharing who, what, where, how, and whys of God. Given the realities of pain and suffering, injustice, war, and loneliness, a movement toward understanding joy has not been a priority.

C. S. Lewis was a profound thinker who taught at Oxford University. In his book, *Surprised by Joy*, he describes joy as a memory and a longing. He wrote that joy is not a possession. Joy is deeply felt. It comes at unexpected times. The experience leaves a lasting impression. Our loving and being loved in deep interpersonal connections brings an atmosphere for joy. In a joy, we feel deeply alive, aware of the love of God. A church or community of joy reaches out to "the least of these." That special ministerial privilege of entering communion with our neighbors holds the potential for joy. Joy is like free-flowing blood pumping into the hearts of people of God who do not numb themselves from the fruit of the Spirit.

Spiritual awareness is encountered in beauty, nature, prayer, work, play, or in those relationships oozing with love. A theology of joy is not denial of social issues. Joy is not involved in any movement that uses a blind eye to ignore human needs. Youth and joyful music says this: "I wish for you, my friend, the happiness that I've found." Joy is something you want to pass on.

Part of my ministry in retirement is to coach depressed pastors, who neglect their wellbeing. Souls are made for endurance. But we lose our vitality and zest. In many congregations during pastoral prayer time, we ask people to share their "joys .and concerns." The "concerns" include sharing of medical problems. They share those divorcing or in trouble. They receive hugs, tears, care, sympathy, condolences, and continuing prayers. Unless solicited by the pastor or worship leader to share their blessings and joys, most congregations become reserved. So, celebrations and joys are abbreviated or even omitted. Sharing momentary joy can be a source of solace for a person who is struggling with negatives and "concerns" could benefit from the experience of vicarious delight for someone else's joy. Congregations lose out on an opportunity to wonder, ponder, rejoice, and honor the Giver of all good gifts. Praises and hymns of joy can mean so much to those living the realities of their lives. Sharing our joys brings important opportunities to discuss a theology of joy. With theological reflection people, might be stimulated to ask questions. They may reflect "Why me? Why have I been so blessed? What am I doing with the talents and gifts God has given me?"

The questions would help people discern the purpose and meaning of our lives. More people of every age will be attracted to attend a congregation that explores experiences of beauty, grace, goodness, strength, radiance, and joy.

If our churches can bring out experiences of joy, then those stories will give God's people a deeper understanding of God's love and God's gifts of joy. No longer will our declining churches continue expressions of despair, despair, hopelessness, and joylessness.

As minister of joy to the world, my goal is to experience more people becoming joyologists. Our ministries of compassion will find that ordinary people can use their spiritual and natural gifts to help the church grow and expand. Ministers are called today to link the experiences of joy to expressions of gratitude to God, and happiness in our communities of faith. Joy is not such a scarce resource to be hoarded or hidden, a positive light hidden under a bushel. Joy is like the loaves and the fishes. When offered up and shared, it will be multiplied.

A person who practices compassion opens large spaces for the joys that connect us to our family, friends, and neighbors show us that we are not alone or limited by the resources we have now. Recently, I attended a workshop on writing called the Fredrick Buechner Seminar held at Princeton University. He is a Presbyterian minister who has used his gift of writing to bless our world.

In his book, Wishful *Thinking: A Theological ABC*, he shares on page 95, "The place God calls you to is the place where your deep gladness and the world's deep hunger meet." Our mainline churches are empty, dying, and closing. However, seminaries and divinity schools have more students than ever. Buechner's view of a calling resonates with students. With fewer churches available, one of our tasks is to help nurture gifted people to serve in global ministries, small rural congregations, or in tent making vocations where there is a deep need. God's gift of joy is not a small thing. The absence of joy is a sign of diminished life. Joy flows from the tender heart of our compassionate God. One of my mentors in my earliest ministry days advised that I be trained to do something else than serving as the pastor of a congregation.

"Church is a difficult and sometimes mean place. They are known to kick you out into the street. Too many are forced to quit," he said. Another random thought shared by Dr. John Killinger: "Joys are like fireflies; they light up the darkness with their flickering brilliance, then die so we can enjoy the other joys that surround us."

Chapter Six
Joylessness of All Generations
in Dying Churches

All generations—babies, children, youth, young adults, and older adults—are missing abundant life. All mainline denominations are now trying to react to declines in membership, Bible study, and worship attendance. Generally, mainline refers to the Episcopal, American Baptist, United Methodists, United Church of Christ, Christian Church (Disciples of Christ) and the Presbyterian Church (USA) are included.

Licensed mental health practitioners are reported a huge rise in mental illness. This is happening in the three stages of life—birth to age 30, age 30-60, and age 60-90. Churches are failing with ministry to and by people in all generations.

Human beings of every age are needed to grasp the realities of the cultures. Some of our older members refuse to see that their length of life, gifts of wisdom, and experience must be used if Christian faith communities are to survive. Every single day, more than 1,000 people celebrate their 70th birthdays. There will be elder adults than any other age group by 2020. More than half of those attending churches today are senior citizens. They are blessed with new and better health, a true radiance. Older adults stroke the fire of faith with ongoing learning which enlivens spiritual values in the way they now live. Their acts of service, counting of blessings, daily praise, and worship show a sincere desire to have intimacy with God. One step toward God leads to another and another. Each day is a new beginning. We are not called to do great things, but we can all do little things with great love. Mother Teresa expressed these words in her teachings and writings. People get caught up in current concepts of church. Love, beauty, and joy come from within. We could never buy them. It comes from an awareness and reliance on God.

It is a societal problem of every day of living to avoid getting sucked into a cultural rut that runs deep and affects every person. Our image of ourselves and of our communities of fate is false and hurtful.

The years of our maturity are not times of dying or declining beauty. And we cannot cling to the past. Everyone was created for a special purpose. God is all around us, calling to us, giving us opportunities to draw closer and drink deeply of God's unconditional love.

Older adults think wrongly if they say the church will die if she is not replenished by young adults and you coming to sit in the pews or chairs. These joyless church people seek to give up their ministry and purpose by giving the ministries to younger people in place of the older folks. Churches have lost the ability to teach Christian faith. Sunday School and Bible study hours take up just about twenty minutes of each hour. Most are boring and are taught by volunteers who merely fill the space. Many adolescents have attended to please parents and grandparents and after confirmation, they never attend church again. Most do not confirm their faith. They have never had a personal relationship with God. They have never danced with God. Ongoing theological reflection was never integrated into their "church activities." Churches are failing in engaging members in discipleship and faith formation. There is a decline not only in church affiliation and connection, but there is a decline in human wellbeing that parallels the decline in spiritual life.

Our age of utter misery and joylessness is filled with ineffective youth and children's leaders. Many children's sermons are made by a person who has no deep faith. The children's sermon is given during worship to ensure attendance. The children leave with some candy, but fail to appreciate God's love and what faith means.
An unforgettable joy that I have about giving the children's sermon was one Sunday when more than 25 kids came running to the front of the sanctuary. I was dressed in my robes. One little girl looked up into my eyes and said, "Are you Jesus?"

Each generation is at greater risk of developing depressive disorders and of seeing the church community die. The world's culture is giving a false picture of human happiness and joy. We are drifting away from the kind of education and resources of previous generations to enable children and youth to find out what makes life worth living. Church is not an attractive place. Church can major on a theology of joy or just wring our hands and exhaust ourselves coping with the consequences, or we can pray and work to find what is going on, why it's going on, how we can turn the tide. Churches must include every age. A warm and nurturing body of Christ must have a long-range plan. Reflecting on God and articulating a theology of joy will help those seeking a connection which is at the core of our identity and purpose of our life on earth. The church as a gathered body of Christ will embrace all generations with grace, unconditional love, beauty, and joy. That result will be astonishing.

"Are you Jesus?" That question continues to haunt me. What will be the foundation of the joy movement? In some ways, we are Jesus. The Kingdom of God is here and now. Jesus lives inside us. The church cannot worship the Holy Scriptures. The Bible is a guide to knowing the God of history and our foundation and human fulfillment in Jesus as the Christ, the Messiah. A theology of joy will invite our questions. The reflections honor Jesus, the Holy Spirit, and God. Because joy is a human emotion experienced by all human beings, all religious or secular communities, some might think they can let go of Jesus. Jesus is the Lord of the dance. We dance best with God when we know the music.

Chapter Seven
Music for the Dance with God

Diane Bish is sharing the joy of music in her third stage of life. She is an organist who travels the world playing music in the great cathedrals and churches around the world. Her books, television shows, and concerts have been a blessing to millions.

Joy is inseparable from the whole fruit of the Spirit. The fruit is not only joy, but love, peace, patience, kindness, goodness, faithfulness, gentleness, and self-control. The musical anthem for dancing with God can be a choral piece from Beethoven's Ninth Symphony called "Ode to Joy."

The church community still maintains that universal joy is humankind's chief end. What does music have to about joy? Music arouses our basic values and taps into our models of joy. "Ode to Joy" along with traditional hymns and today's praise music sounds as if it is bringing our world into being. The narrative ends with a complete atmosphere for joy with the people of God united in song with the famous D major tune.

What does joy sound like? Karl Barth, theologian, was infatuated with Mozart. Wolfgang Amadeus Mozart produced beautiful music. The music of Mozart affirms that God is good. God is love.

In his theological reflections, Clement of Alexandria envisions the music of the spheres in the image of Christ as the new song. Clement's vision quest for music involves the redeeming singing with Christ Jesus with all of creation sounding out musically the relationship to and with God. The music of the spheres is music that hears the entire creations of God under the care and power of God.

Music is alive as joy is. My wife and I sensed this truth as we enjoyed the "Magic Flute," the clarinet concerto of October 1791. Mozart died in a state of joylessness. His is an unknown grave. The music of Charles Wesley set the fire for the Wesleyan movement. His songs were composed with the tunes heard in the common bars among ordinary people.

My concept of joy includes an emotion in relation to some person, encounter, or object. One piece of the model is that joy desires to be shared. Joy originates in and is part of the love shared between our triune God. Indeed, Jesus, God, and the Holy Spirit dance together in mutual love. The church has always encountered this joyful dance of love by way of worship. Within the music and the sacraments, the Kingdom of God is realized. A special joy is shared for me every time I baptize a new professing Christian. Nothing compares to the joy of a young and zealous new believer receiving God's gift of love. With smiles they are invited to the joyous dance of a new creation. It is always an honor to be witness to a child of God surrendering their lives to God.

In my long ministerial career, I baptized several thousand persons. In Missouri, I baptized a man who was 98 years old. A little boy who was reluctant to go under the water, tightened his lips and was witness to the death, burial, and resurrection to new life. One young adult began singing as she entered the pool. Some said she sounded like an angel. Her musical confession led to more joy. Her response was quite fitting with praise, thanksgiving, and her warm reception into the Kingdom of God.

On the journey of a lifetime newly born into Spirit recognizes and feels intimacy with God. The joys are multiplied and returned by the same God who is the source. The adolescent has a pump primed for joy. Their passionate cognitive development is more intense than it is with children. These youths are ripe for reflection. My grandson Ethan tells me of a time for a joy while on a trip to the mountains in Maine. They hiked through the mountains in southern Maine. His experience with his dad demonstrated self-transcendence that evokes joy. Young people discover joy when playing sports, singing in a musical group, or other ventures with other youth. That's one reason music should be taught in our schools. My brother David and his wife Cindy played in the University of Tennessee marching band. They enjoyed pep bands, concerts, and just funning around. Playing songs such as "Rocky Top" they found themselves caught up the power of the music. The more than 107,000 fans of the Tennessee Volunteers were also caught up especially when the Vols scored a dramatic touchdown. For the college students, these were the first tastes of joy.

Young people who readily share a joy are already primed for receiving "the joy of the Lord." Most youth develop a passion for music in worship. In recent years, The Church has fought the so-called music wars. At first it was only the independent or low church communities that sang only praise or hard rock music. It was like attending a secular rock concert. Mainline congregations followed suit by buying worship screens and playing videos of praise music alongside traditional hymns. Soon youth led worship was like an ecstatic concert. If the concert was allowed in the church building, hundreds, even thousands of youth from everywhere would attend. The over 30 crowd rarely attended.

Other congregations would invite country and western style singers such as the Blackwood Brothers that drew the older people. Country gospel appeals to the 30-60 age audience and especially that 60-90. People will travel 200miles to hear the old-time gospel singing. They come alive as they listen to old favorite bluegrass ballads and songs such as "Drop Kick Me Jesus Through the Goal Posts of Life."

Any style of music can enable people to reflect on God. Each musical style is a gift to the church. Churches should continue to sponsor retreats and camp experiences for youth. These settings become outposts of hope, where young people, by participating in Christian life in a natural setting. While their youth sense the redemptive activity of God in their lives. During a summer youth camp in Erwin, Tennessee, I responded to my call into ministry. After the youth go back home again, camp events become benchmarks by which the rest of a child's life is measured and interpreted. The theology of joy reflects the overflowing love of God. God is singing, "May I have this dance for the rest of your life."

Joy is never experienced in isolation. Joy is the emotion that causes our hearts to sing. Joy brings self-confidence, self-acceptance, and a deep knowing that our existence is not viewed with indifference. In loving ourselves, we are more likely to feel acceptance by the world. As a child, did you sing and laugh when you were in a time of joy? Remember the family trips, Christmas celebrations, birthdays, and accomplishments that aroused joy inside of you. Remember the first time you experienced being in love. Recall the conversation with a dying parent about what brought joy in their past. Did you notice a change in their face, in their tendency to feel like a child again?

During our last years of life, we lose ourselves into the past. We continue to gaze at old photos as we are drawn to the richness of the accumulated life experience. So, we celebrate who we are and the ways our lives have been blessed by each other.

My musical wife sang the old song," My Work Is Done" as her mother breathed her last breath. A young girl once asked her Dad, "How do you sing the sad songs of life?" God encounters each of us, in every phase of our lives, in a song overflowing with love.

God sings and dances with us throughout our brief days, much like we coo to our new born babies. They may not understand, but that music in our souls bathes their souls in love. God's tender attention to us is sung during our experiences, in our relationships, and during our efforts to listen. God can bring good out of every moment as we hear his words. These words are. words to the music when we dance with God.

Chapter Eight
Searchlights and Flashlights:
Happiness and Joy

For more than 50 years of preaching, teaching, writing, coaching, and counseling as Minister of Joy to the World, I have used the illustration that a joy experience is like a flashlight that comes in a momentary event. Happiness is like a searchlight involving all the emotions of a lifetime. Happiness is more of the state of life perceived as good.

Our theological understanding of happiness means different things to many people. Psychologists and scholars in the positive psychology movement have used research methods to answer questions about what happiness is and how it is attained and described. That research has revealed that happiness is a description of human well-being, perhaps closer to overall contentment including times of intense joy.

Happy people are both emotionally, physically, and spiritually healthier than unhappy ones. There is also clear evidence that a person can increase the level of happiness with actions like exercising. to release endorphins. Eating well also contributes to happiness. Many serious diseases can be avoided by good nutrition. Scientists view mood disorders such as depression have no single cause. Models by biological, psychological, and sociological, and theological scholars show multiple causes to the human life being viewed as healthy.

Human beings try to do things that will cause them to be happy. They acquire money, envied educations, an expensive automobile, or a big custom built dream house. None of these things prove to increase the levels of happiness.

Politicians, world travelers, or ordinary people who win a huge lottery are no happier than those who do not experience any of these things in their lifetimes. External and material things that come into a life journey may cause happiness for some people who attain them for temporarily, but they soon revert to their baseline level. Challenges for daily living, training for the limited ones who do not attend college, or develop some skills to buy, food, shelter, and clothing. The searchlight that reveals all our emotions, highs and lows, opportunities or environment of no chance, even genetics are involved for happiness.

Joy is more light a flashlight shining on one event such as a positive connection with other people, with nature, by appreciation for learning, a natural flow in appreciating art and music. A joy requires accepting life as it is. Life includes joys and sorrows, abundance and lack. Life does not always treat us well. An untimely death, financial devastation, crime and terror, illness, divorce, growing older, or becoming disabled are the base of transitions that come. into one's life. Every human will face these aspects of life until we die. A joy experience comes as a surprise. Nobody can create or choose a joy. Joy comes and stores the memory of the experience that can alter negative attitudes on life. Joy times yield a sense of wellbeing.

Joy arrives as a gift to soothe the sorrowful times and agonizing disasters. Happiness is an attitude in our hearts, our souls, our spirits that enables us to cope with the challenges that bring stress and. strain. Ancient and modern views of happiness admit that nobody is happy all the time. It is one's overall look at life which brings inner peace and contentment. Joy brings on a smile. It is a time of reality not fantasy. Being grateful for what one has or is increases the happiness level. Content people are thankful for their jobs, health, family, home, and status. Workers may experience joy if they receive a bonus or. special award or meaningful gift or promotion. Getting a regular pay check every month does not cause the arousal of joy. Joy is expressed in a community. Sharing the experience brings on celebration.

We may experience joy if our physician gives us a clean bill of health. Joy comes with a job offer with a cherished company. It is a joy for some when a marriage proposal is accepted. Those experiences will be. inside our brains never to be forgotten. That memory will have happened even if you doctor failed to detect a life-threatening illness. The joy of love and the nightmare of your partner walking away before there is a wedding. The new job opportunity becomes a disaster. So, these joys prove to be based on positive facts and expectations. Staying motivated when the going gets tough is not easy. It is a challenge for any person who desires to create a meaningful life. Overnight successes are extremely rare. We see the end results of happy and well known and accomplished people. Hardly ever do we discuss the difficulties, the frustrations, and the dark days along the journey.

Those who flourish do so because they stayed focused on their goals, deal with the setbacks, and hang in there. They also pay attention to synchronicity, enlist support, take care of themselves, and create their own luck. They persist because they see purpose for their lives and do what they love.

Visualizations of what happiness looks like to you will help. As a coach. and a counselor, I ask, "What would it look like if your problem was solved? Writing affirmations are helpful as we list our goals. Encouraging words and affirmations with visualizations have enabled people to find a job, travel to Europe, meet a friend, and even the exact date they want to begin.

In therapy sessions, I have people to close their eyes and visualize what they Want. They close their eyes and see themselves being in a desired setting. They are doing what they love to do—writing a book, painting a picture, playing music, dancing. They see the colors, hear the sounds, smell the flowers, and touch the beauty. Some might even write about that visualization in their journal as if the experience is continuing to happen.

Afterward, they will be aware of synchronistic events or information that will support what is in your journal. When a person is clear about the intention and focuses the life energy and action toward the results desired, joy and miracles will happen. Isolation is a dream killer. Let friends and those empowered to help you. Hire a counselor or a life coach. Life is hard enough without help. No one does anything alone. All humans are interdependent. We need each other. Keep the search light of happiness glowing. We are each other's champions as well as representatives in the world. Every member of your family, congregation, conference or region, and friends have ties to. the world. They will prod you on and help you heal any wounds or obstacles that prevent you from reaching your goals. Remember, we need each other. Life is just too difficult to do it alone. Scripture tells us to "have this mind in you that is the mind of Christ.". We have limited power over our minds. The mind is always planning, thinking, assessing, and projecting. No human being can just not think.

Thoughts come and go and continually affect our emotions and feelings. Our thoughts have a life of their own. They influence our physical and emotional reactions. Close your eyes and imagine a lemon. See the bright yellow color. See its oval shape. Smell its sweet smell. Drink the juice straight from the lemon. Pucker your mouth. Taste the sourness. All this because you. thought about a lemon. A thought can arouse an emotion. Thoughts make you sad. They make stomachs upset. Shoulders and backs stiffen. Thoughts keep people in unhealthy behavioral patterns, bad relationships, painful jobs, continuing misery because they fear something worse will happen if they act differently. People become comfortable with discomfort, think about it, and then just remain miserable.

Write down what you want to do. Then write what will happen if you do not act to accomplish what it is you want. If you continue to do. what you are now doing and feeling what you are now feeling, what. is the worst possible situation that will occur and then what? How will it affect your relationships, your health, and your own self? If we keep doing what we've done as a family, a church, or as a nation, we'll keep getting what we now have. Changing direction or repenting leads. to happiness. Do work you love. Keep expanding your natural talents and your passions. Use them now for your time living on earth is brief and limited. Everything you can imagine is subject to loss. Your family, your job,

Your house, your health, and your very life on earth ends quicker than we think. Older people who have lived long lives get in touch with the big picture. Most choose to be happy and to accept ultimate reality. We change and grow from within us as the Kingdom of God is realized on earth and. in heaven. God does not create us to tease our appetites and test our endurance. The Spirit enables us to see the face of God in every day we live on this earth. Each day is a gift, a treasure to be cherished one day at a time. A Higher Power is in control on our dark as well as. the light days. Consider it all "very good," as God tells us.

Chapter Nine
Jesus Came to Bring Joy and Happiness to a World Starved for Love

A theology of joy and happiness must begin with Jesus. Holy Scriptures tell us about the Son of God. If Jesus is the touchstone, then we must deal with. the teachings he shared. Jesus called for and lived thirty-three years of. awareness and dependence upon God. Born as a helpless baby, Jesus lived the kind of life expected of all sons and daughters of God. Jesus' life and ours ends with a cross. He lived. in constant danger and rejection. His life ended in an awful death at the hands of the reigning empire.

The New Testament writers were realistic about the consequences of following Jesus. His birth shaped the theology of God and God's relationship to the people of Israel and the whole world. Jesus lived out a model that identifies how any inhabitant on earth was to live the life journey as a citizen of the kingdom of God. Jesus lives today. All other religious leaders have died and none of them has a personal intimate relationship with God as Christians do. They celebrate rituals such as those who follow Islam pray five times daily. Secular culture praises the living of life by your own power. Abraham Maslow use the term self-realization. A long book, even an encyclopedia could not satisfy our search for happiness or joy. A young person could care less about what Karl Barth or any scholar must say when the parents are in the middle of a nasty divorce. In seminary students give enough energy to pass the courses, but not enough to deal with reality.

A theology of joy is not found by reading commentaries, scholarly journals, but is best understood as God works with us each day. Most of our lifelong search leads us to the model lived by Jesus. In later chapters, we will focus on the explanations about joy in the Hebrew Scriptures and in the Christian New Testament. The scriptures bear witnesses to the world and to humankind. Christ is the source of all that exists. Secular historians know of Jesus' in a historical time and place. He is identified as a Galilean Jew. He interpreted the Torah and. challenged the Pharisees. He died on a cross. Jesus told us and his disciples of the first century to follow him in his journey. The result was to be peace, rest, joy, and an abundance filled life.

So, humans live in Christ. Jesus said the kingdom is within us. Scripture calls for people to follow the Way with kindness, patience, peace, thanksgiving, hospitality, giving, and joy. Living in the kingdom of God means doing the practices and dispositions that we learn from Jesus and the pattern of his life. This mysterious fellowship with Jesus is understood from his brief life on earth. Christ is the image of God. Humans and all there is, was created by God, and we confess that Jesus is an exact blueprint of God's being. God in Christ. and the Holy Spirit sustains the creation including every person who has lived on the earth. How earth ends, or perhaps begins again is within the authority of Jesus the Christ. Within a theology of joy, we visualize the. end at the beginning as Steven Covey has said. Words such as new life, eternal life, new birth, new creation are descriptions of renewed existence in the image of the Creator. Being made new, we are already living in the kingdom of God. So, as Kingdom citizens we will participate when God is the power and glory as God is in heaven.

As death and sin and evil end, the children of God will receive the benefits or the rewards. All of history—past years, present time, and the future—belong to God in Christ. Every child of God was created in a world that God called "very good.". Humans are not just passive dwellers but caretakers of God's "very good" earth. Our world is holy ground. If human interdependence is destroyed, earth becomes not a home, but a threat. People were created to be. together, not lonely or alone. In the Revelation of John of Patmos, these singing at the throne of God will be from every race and every nation.

Joy will be the dominant emotion. There will be no more tears, no more death. All creation will be dancing in the city of Light. Human beings come into fullness in Christ. (Col. 2:10) We anticipate an existence when God will be "all in all." (I Cor. 15:28) To know the love of Christ we are filled with the fullness of God. (Eph. 3:19).

In later chapters, we shall ponder the Old Testament's ideal of joy. God in Jesus overcame the power of sin. Meanwhile, those who live in the circumstances of earth today are not yet fully saved from earth's groaning and decay. Guilt, anger, anxiety, and fear prevail in our present age. Those moments of joy that we experience on earth will be stretched and multiplied in heaven. We will enjoy the fullness of the new creation. In our worship and in our work, we are filled with hope and anticipation of God's new creation. In John, we read the phrase "abundant life.". (John 10:10) Life and eternal life are in John's thinking to be lived and enjoyed while we are still living on the earth. "Abundant life" anticipates the resurrection life with God fill with joy and hope. When Jesus says, "Follow me," what does he mean? He means to trust and believe him. He means physically walking beside him.

"Come unto me" includes Jesus' teachings about the kingdom of God, the place for the law, and how to live with each other. His teaching causes the world to say, "He was a great teacher, but not our Lord and Master, Christ, or Messiah." On one occasion, the disciples wanted Jesus to teach them to pray. He did hours of praying. Just being with him made prayers to rely on God's help and direction. They had seen Jesus forgive sin. Miracles of healing were experienced when Jesus forgave people their sins. The disciples wanted to know just how many times they must do the same. The men and the women disciples were to participate and receive the kingdom of God. They saw the kingdom lived first hand. They were the first witnesses of the present and coming kingdom. With the mind and person of Christ living inside of them, they preached and taught, and healed by the power of love. They were so full of love and grace that they ate with sinners, tax collectors, and "the least of them" as Jesus had done. The followers of Jesus became spiritually aware and fully alive. Jesus' vision of the kingdom of God not just returning the world to what it was but to the intention of creation. The kingdom is a gift. (Luke 12:42) It is entered with joy. Jesus speaks of the joy of completing the work of God. God's joy was expressed when he delightfully called his creation "very good.".

Jesus expressed a "rejoicing in the Holy Spirit" when the disciples gave their report on their mission. Church community gatherings rarely experience joy when they receive the annual report, the state of the region, charge conference, and other gatherings such as the one when Jesus heard what the. ordinary disciples had accomplished when being filled with the Holy Spirit. (Luke 10:21)

When we are faithful, maybe not successful, we enter into "the joy of. the Master." (Matt. 13:20; 25:21-23) That joy is experienced in a. moment in time, in the presence of a community, and warmed by anticipation of more joy to come. And as my mentor says, "Every joy is preparation for the next one. "From the joyful day when parents and others are in a time of joy until our day of our death, our lives are filled with securing, obtaining, building, getting, owning. Jesus teaches a new way of living that involves losing, letting go, relinquishing what one has, and what one is in relation with God.

When Jesus taught that people must seek the kingdom, he is not asking them to find what is hidden and unattainable. The kingdom of God comes as a gift, a pearl of great price, a treasure buried in a field. The response to that gift is joy.

Close your eyes and visualize Jesus. See him eat with tax collectors, with outsiders, and those judged to be sinners. See him raise the dead. Observe his welcome of a weeping woman sitting at his feet. Hear him ask God to forgive his executioners.

The disciples of Christ imitate Jesus. They participate in his work. It is no wonder that when these early disciples returned from their mission, they returned with joy. (Luke 10:17) The cost of discipleship is not cheap, but steep. The cost is high indeed. John's gospel ends with Jesus telling Peter that Peter can expect to follow Jesus to his own death. With Christ inside us, we live with a peace that is beyond understanding and the very joy that Jesus has (John 15:11, 17:13) So if Jesus is the model for living, his life was full of gratitude, trust, and giving of self all for God's glory. His story is filled with love. One cannot trust a. God who does not love. We are invited to play a part in this story. Those on whom the love of God has poured into their souls are also to love. Those on whom the Holy Spirit works joy are to rejoice. (Phil. 4:4-7).

Participation in the work of God's kingdom brings joy and hope. A theology of joy invites us to life with the power who sustains all humankind and that life is not lived by bread alone. God's power is that power of peace, love, and joy.

Theological reflection leaves the resolution of "all things" to the one who made all things. Part of living by faith is rooted in the desire for a new Eden. Perhaps that is what my beloved professor Dr. John Killinger was expressing when he said," When I get to the point where I don't enjoy my life, it is time for me to die into another world of joy."

Chapter Ten
Journeys with Joy and
Strength in the Lord

In 1996, I went to share some vision quests for joy in a church in Edinburgh, Scotland. A noted repertory theater group performed one Saturday, and the church was packed. The performance began with a humorous play. No one laughed. And then a young woman gave a funny parody about church. Again, nobody laughed. Near the end, the director of the program said, "These people must hate. us. There is not even a smile in the huge audience."

Following the performance there was a reception with coffee or tea and. biscuits. Biscuits are cookies in Scotland. The troupe was puzzled when everyone told them how much they enjoyed the evening. One huge jolly-looking chap said, "It was hard not to laugh in church.". One of the reasons the mainline churches are declining and dying in the United States and Europe is that people have disassociated joy and. gladness from church. People endure church, but few create an atmosphere. where joy and miracles happen. For these Scottish Christians and for today, people associate joy and gladness with the pub. If Christ lives inside of us, and the kingdom of God is "entering the joy of the Lord," then "the joy of the Lord is our strength." (Neh. 8:8-12) Nehemiah, Ezra and several scribes read the Scriptures from dawn until noon. People were weeping as they repented when they realized they had failed God. Nehemiah encouraged them not to mourn, but to enjoy the feast for "the joy of the Lord is our strength."

Christians must seek to know experientially the joy of the Lord, which will create spiritual strength. As I shared with my grandson Ethan, God does not expect us to always be dancing like the bouncy Tigger. But with Christ guiding us, we cannot be glum and sad like Eeyore.

Followers of Christ can experience joy anywhere. One of my goals as "minister of joy to the world" is to share the joy of the Lord with people in every nation and territory of the world. Stories of joy can be found in many places, but Christian mission fields are full of intriguing stories. As you come to know real mission work and missionaries, you observe the demise of the stereotype of pith-helmeted, culturally intensive religious go getters. Laurel and I enjoy staying in the homes of missionaries. An advantage for us also is that our daughters are married to career military men who travel the world on behalf of the United States army. Most of the missionaries have been dedicated women and men fueled by love.

For two years, I served on the regional board of the Christian Church (Disciples of Christ) in Nebraska as the representative for Global Missions. There is amazing work being accomplished on mission fields. Medical nurses and doctors work hand in hand on mission fields with ministers and evangelists. Some commit to missions from some of the best medical schools such as Harvard, Vanderbilt, Stanford, Yale, and state university schools of medicine. Some spend their lives in backwater towns in poor and struggling nations and territories throughout the world.

These men and women chose to serve where God needed them rather than gain the money and power they could have in the United States. Some even risk their health and their lives by serving in disease-infested parts of the world. Why do they sacrifice so much? As one University of. Tennessee Medical Units graduate serving in Zaire told me, without a bit of hesitation, "Love for the people and my strength in the joy of the Lord." Love lasts.

Moments of being in a joy motivate people to choose a calling and a place to serve that few would ever consider. The brick, mortar, and steel in our church buildings will be gone. We see it everywhere in cities and rural areas. Ground once considered as holy are now abandoned as more than 1,000 churches close every week. Church buildings are now being torn down to make room for high-rise buildings. People meet in houses, barns, bars, school buildings, anywhere that people can gather. Trained ordained. pastors serve churches for free and make their living in a secular tent-. making profession such as medicine, law, or any other money-making work.

As people go on a strategic spiritual journey and walk more closely with God, they do not overlook the strong resources from the Lord. God's love is always there in joyful or joyless times. Once one experiences the love and joy, the person pours forth the overflow to family, friends, acquaintances, strangers, and to those with needs throughout the world. Inside of each soul is God's own caring. God came in Jesus with a demonstration of the Lord's intense love for every person on earth. When we pray to Jesus, we are reminded of that love. Study of the historic, biblical, and scientific records of the early church, shows that they sensed a living presence of Jesus.

First Peter communicates a special happiness atmosphere. "Though you have not seen him, you love him and you believe in him and are filled with inexpressible and glorious joy. (I Peter 1:8, NIV) The spirit gave them peace. People nearby could see it. Those living around them understood that in the times of troubles facing these Christians, and there were plenty of problems for them, these people had a deep sense of well-being. that was reflected on every inch of their countenances. If we are to renew our dying congregations, we must share the joy. that the early church experienced. This will require our focus to be not on sports, pleasures, and other priorities that have caused spiritual death. Christ is real to those who commit everything to our highest values. Jesus is not an abstraction to be analyzed. He is not just one historic figure to be left in the ancient past. He is our contemporary source of strength. With loyalty to Christ, we continue to express his thoughts and discover our moods change and we are surprised by joy. Joy touches us throughout our brief journey on earth.

A surgeon experiences a moment of accomplishment as she completes a lifesaving procedure. Intense joy surrounds a mother who first holds her new born. A child slips into sheer joy while building a sand castle on the beach on a sunny summer day. As the child brushes sand from the legs, feet, and hands, they run to find daddy and mommy to share their achievement. The child's face radiates. It is the nature of humans to talk about joy. Most do not understand it. They never reach the awareness that joy requires a satisfaction of the soul, not just the mind. Mental comprehension or even studies in a laboratory cannot bring the fulfilling moments of the "joy of the Lord." Neither can possession of objects, power, and achievements result in happiness.

Joy is being, not knowing or having. The warm glow of a human soul, the freedom from guilt and shame, fear and anxiety, are the ultimate criterion for joy. She no longer feels like an alien, but rejoices in the freedom as a beloved child of God.

The result of all our writing, research, preaching and teaching is an undercurrent, a firm foundation that comes from being just who we all and knowing that all is well. "It is well; it is well with my soul."

Serious research reveals the fear that grips our youth. Pippa danced with the cosmos and sang, "God's in his heaven, all's right with the world." In our day, young people sing, "The bomb is on the horizon, all's wrong with the world."

In our restoration of the things that were real and the strength of the early church. Those filled with that "joy of the Lord" will have inner strength to remain calm, assured, and even joyful. Nuclear bombs are the most destructive that humans have created, but those with the "mind of

Christ" know life is still controlled by God. God is. guiding the future of his creation.

God loved humankind enough to become incarnate and live among us. The Creator did not stay distant and communicate from away out there. When you know God cares that much, you can build an atmosphere upon which to rest your soul.

When we think about Jesus' time on earth, we observe the hallmarks of the calm and joy which was his strength. Joy is a vital part of the. earthly journey. Peaks of immense joy are not unique to Christians' every human experience and every emotion. What differs for those "in Christ" is the anticipation for joy every day. Tapping the strength of the Lord's joy adds richness and fullness to life. We can look to Jesus as our role model and guide. The joy he demonstrated in life and death was a constant outpouring of walking with God.

Chapter Eleven
Joy at the Beginning and End
of the Cosmic Dance

"Go out in joy and be led forth in peace; the mountains and hills will burst forth into song before you." (Isaiah 55:12). The Roman Catholic author and priest Thomas Merton has said, "No. despair of ours can alter the reality of things, or stain the joy of the cosmic dance which is always there. Indeed, we are in the midst of it, and it is in the midst of us, for it beats in our very blood, whether we want it to or not."

We cannot diminish God's love for us. Our life journey is when we learn how to be aware of it, receive it, trust it, and celebrate it in the whirling invitation to join in the cosmic dance.

Body, soul, and mind are involved as we dance. Play or listen to. music that moves you. It can be gospel, country, folk, jazz, contemporary, traditional, or classical. Find a place where you can listen and move with no inhibitions.

Allow your body to lead, following the inviting sound of the music. Give the rational mind a seat. Tune into the sensations of every part of your body. Feel your feet pounding on the surface of the ground. Enjoy your swing and sway as you move your head, hips, arms, and shoulders. Dance until you are tired. In the end just relax and sit down in the silence.

Reflect on this prayer by an unknown writer read by an elder in the worship at First Christian Church in Pawnee City, Nebraska.

> "Giver of life, creator of all that is lovely, teach me to sing the words your song; I want to feel he music of living and not fear the sad songs. But from them make new songs. Composed of both laughter and tears. Teach me to dance to the sounds of your world. And your people. I desire to move in rhythm with your plan, help me to try to follow your leading. To risk even falling.
>
> To rise and keep trying. Because you are leading the dance.".

Joy can co-exist with doubt and uncertainty, during times of pain and confusion. The journey with joy is muffled, detoured, a mystery in. which we participate, not a product we can grasp. We must let go and trust. the leader of the dance. As the years pass by, we become aware that failures and difficulties are a critical part of life, and are our opportunities to grow.

When we give up our need for security, for everything to be right, then the peace that passes understanding has room to quietly come into our lives again. Many may know the name and life of Jesus, but most continue to live without Jesus. It is a tragedy that some people are too familiar with him in the sense that they think they know and think they understand all things about the significance of his life within and among us.

No person can comprehend Jesus. The joy times he would give are different from what we think it is. A remarkable thing about joy is that his single emotion integrates the dimensions of the good life. Joy is not just a pleasurable feeling, but it is the most pleasurable emotion. It is aroused in us when life goes well. Joy comes as a surprise even when we are suffering. Joy is not a description of. the whole of good life, but one moment only.

People miss the unexpected joy because they have preconceived images of what joy is supposed to be. Instead of taking the time and energy it takes to dig in to find a theology of joy, they cling to those experiences they disillusion themselves, and keep on preserving a false joy.

As I attempt to be a small part of the joy movement as I coach, teach, write and preach healthy change, I too am changed. My preconceived theology with my images about life, about God, about others, and about myself have helped me to imagine that we are much more than we think. Life is constantly new, different, changing, and far more powerful than any ideal I had ever dreamed about. The pain in my personal journey and that of my family and friends has been all too real, but so has the joy.

The seemingly impossible happens every day. On the first of October, 2016, the University of Tennessee football team saw themselves behind 17-0 in a game with the University of Georgia Bulldogs in Athens, Georgia. In the beginning of the second half, it looked like the Volunteers would not do anything different. They had come from behind in every game as they defeated Appalachian State, Ohio University, and even the Florida Gators, a team the Vols had not beaten in many years.

Tennessee had challenging defensive stands. They even recovered. fumble in the end one of Georgia to miraculously take the lead for the first time. Kicking to Georgia, the game appeared to be in the hands of Tennessee. Deep in the Georgia side of the field, the quarterback keeps successfully moving the ball. When the game was near the end, the Bulldog field general heaved a long touchdown pass that left the fans of Georgia acting out emotions of delight. As they kicked the extra point, only ten seconds were left on the official time clock. After the ball was kicked to Tennessee, fans of Tennessee showed disappointment. With only four seconds left, the Volunteers had managed on. the first play to get the ball across the Georgia 50-yard line. There was only four seconds left. Tennessee took their last time out. The coach and players anxiously decided about what kind of play to call. The field goal kicker did not have the ability to kick a football almost 65 yards. Four seconds is not time for two plays. Tennessee had a mathematical .001 change of winning.

The quarterback stepped back with time ran out. Then he tossed the ball longer than he had ever attempted in his career to the receiver who had five Bulldog players surrounding him. They do not call this desperate pass a "hail Mary" for nothing. As the miracle catch happened, Tennessee won the game, 34-31. Each human season, each event in our personal, family, sports, church, and community life sharpens the possibilities and underlines the uniqueness of it all. Every child of God has her own story. God created none of us alike.

Ken Caraway said," There is no box made by God nor us, but that the sides can be flattened and the top blown off to build a dance floor on which to celebrate life." Despite our many limitations, our goal is to have God guide us on the right path. How do we hear the voice of God? Spend time listening for God's words. God is in the renewal business. The church and all of us can be changed. One of the exciting things about joy is that it can be restored. Our situation may have only a .001 per cent chance, but nothing is impossible with God. "Oh Lord, restore me to the joy of thy salvation." (Psalm 51:12)

There is a new restoration movement afloat now. This joy will be more than repair like dents on an automobile. It is a completely new way for traveling the way from beginning to the ending. In Christ, we can be renewed together as new creatures. For the faithful, this is a picture of happiness, not merely a once in a lifetime moment.

Courage is a human that has said its prayers. Courage is to accept. ourselves and love ourselves as we are created. It does take courage to forget ourselves in recklessly loving a hurting world with the unlimited love of Christ. "The Lord is my shepherd," and I shall not want for joy. Each joy moment is a comforting sign of the presence of the Lord. My cup runs over and I am bathed with the oil of gratitude.

Eternity is beyond comprehension. Most of us do not dwell on eternity. I am just thankful eternity is in God's control and not mine. Eternity began for me when my first commitment and connection was made with Jesus. That connection has no ending. As the psalm writer has said," The Lord is my shepherd so I shall not want forever." Joy often comes during the most difficult circumstances. God's Spirit is more powerful than our own wills. "The joy of the Lord" is greater than our flesh, greater than our guilt or our pain and suffering. With that joy the children of God will experience Christ living today. Our impossible times will be used for us to grow into God's image. Few of us would desire to repeat every moment on our journey. Still, I cannot imagine what my life would be without the sad times as well as the glad times. What if a long movie could be made of every second of our lives? Would we want to see it?

The assets have outnumbered the liabilities, the losses, the pain, the wrong choices, and bad decisions. If I needed to made an honest confession, I do not if I could have the courage, ever want to attempt to live another lifetime journey. It is comforting to know the words of the psalmist, "You have changed my sadness into a joyful dance."

Chapter Twelve
Discovering Joy in Scripture

When I taught the Psychology of Joy at Missouri Western State University in Saint Joseph, my assignments for students was simply to write as paper, prepare some art, or anything that describes your understanding of joy.

One student listed all the verses in Scripture that referred to joy. She then wrote random thoughts on each reference. "After I did this. project, I am more confused as ever." Her evangelical friends had told her that a real Christian has joy all the time. She noted," My understanding of. joy is not constant exoneration and celebration all the time. Life is tough for me. I live with stress, disappointment, heartache, and pain. This is the human condition."

Reading the Psalms reveals that the joy experience comes with religious life. Joy is a significant theme of the Hebrew Scriptures. As we scan the Old Testament, the reality of joy is present without the word joy. My student had copied every instance of joy or rejoicing in her concordance, but she missed a complete view of joy. For example, David's dance for joy comes when the Philistines are defeated and the Ark of God is paraded before the people. (II Sam. 5-6) David's exuberant wild dancing triggers a rebuke from Saul's daughter.

Joy as used in our scriptures is physical. People caught up "in a joy," may use food, wine, dancing, music, and giving of gifts. The Hebrew restoration after the Babylonian exile.

Joy and weeping naturally poured out as the second temple was built. (Ezra 3: 10-13) As an emotion scientific study and religious scriptures, joy is always a result of something seen as a good thing. Anything perceived as good improper relation to an actual and real positive affective response to a life well lived.

My own interpretation of the Bible is that it is a guide to the good life. However, scripture shows that some segments of life, or even most of human lives are negative filled with suffering and hurt, death and dying. with sickness, sin, and much crying out. But through God's love and care, the Lord of the dance turns the mourning into dancing, and our sackcloth into joy." (Psalm 30:11)

Psalm 126 describes joy as a time when "Our mouth was filled with laughter, and our tongue with shouts of joy." Isaiah 9 reflects this understanding. In 9:3 this scripture reads, "You have multiplied the nation, you have increased its joy; they rejoice before you as with joy at the harvest, as people exult when dividing plunder."

The biblical theology of joy includes hope that is often deferred or wiped out day after day, year after year, as the people of God still held onto the hope that how God acted in the past would come to be repeated once again. The Jews held on tightly to the stories told from generation to generation of God leading and restoring the hopes and dreams.

For the early church, the songs held a theme of joy. There was, of course the ongoing hope and anticipation of new interventions by God. In the New Testament writings, the older understanding of who. God is, how God acts, and was making all things new, clear, and focusing on Jesus. So, we can read the saga of what the early followers of the way said about the reasons for a new theology of joy. This includes the angelic joy to be shared with all people at the birth of Jesus in the beginning to the Revelation of the joy when the kingdom of God comes in the ending. (Revelation 19: 6-7)

Jesus reveals the "joy in heaven" when a sinner changes or repents. That is the theme of Luke 15. The theology of joy in the Christian scriptures was taught and preached and lived wherever he went. Jesus demonstrated God's healing, what happiness looked like (the Sermon on the Mount) as he rescued people not from Egypt or Babylon as in the past, but from death. In John's gospel, as in Luke, the reason for joy is that certain things are taking place "on earth as in heaven." Paul writes of joy in his letters. He uses the Greek words for joy throughout including joy and love as the fruit of the Spirit. The Holy Spirit creates the atmosphere or the environment for this fruit to show in the lives of people.

Paul's letter to the Philippians is his most enlightening epistle. concerning joy. Living in a dank Roman prison, his circumstances are full of pain, suffering, and anxiety. Like a retired pastor looking at photos of past pastorates, Paul rejoices in where his earthly journey has taken him. Paul and his Philippi friends loved each other. Paul's theology of joy is found in the heart of this letter. In chapter two, verses 6-11, he shares a poem about Jesus. Paul uses the thoughts of Second Isaiah where we are told of God's victories over pagan gods. Jesus is Lord. No power on earth can bring the salvation that God in Jesus brings. Paul's theology of joy does not mean a spiritual. exhilaration or the leaving of the world and going to a better place. His is not the joy of the Gnostics who yearned for a special knowledge based on reason. The kingdom of God has come. This new kingdom is now happening in the very time of the present, old, corrupt and decaying world.

Paul reveals the cosmic dance of the old world and the new. clashing together, so that the followers of Christ now live between the two. In the immortal Romans 8, he interprets the groaning of all creation as the birth pain of the new world coming into existence.

Scripture insists that the Christ or the Messiah is superior to the thoughts of all the world's religions. Muslims, Hindus, native Americans, Buddhists, or nature followers can never know the power of the resurrection of God in Jesus. Joy is inward strength, not outward show. The wild celebrations of pagan religions are not restrained and the pleasures of loud rock-cultural music and shaking of arms and legs in sensual dancing replace the dignity and deeper meaning of Christian ordinances such as baptism or the holy communion which as Paul wrote "bring unity to the church."

In the Acts of the Apostles, the evils, the persecution, and the multitude of ways and gods associated with Athens and other leading cities of the biblical era.

As my student of the psychology of joy found, a theology of joy might not be present is words translate as joy or rejoice, but we must focus on passages where joy is the main theme. Jesus is the foundation for creating a theology of joy from study of the scriptures. The second coming of Jesus is still to take place. Those who deny the bodily resurrection of Jesus find themselves between the proverbial rock and a hard place in teaching and preaching a theology of joy.

Some sincere and informed scholars do not believe in the ascension. of Jesus into heaven. Obviously, readers of scripture can find all sorts of ideas that turn into unchanging doctrines which keep human beings into darkness as the 40,000 sects of the Christian faith alone clearly show. And so, nobody can come up with a theology of joy or a theology of any theme in early Christian thought and life as there remains continuities and discontinuities. The early Christians had. humble and honest belief that had its beginning in the Hebrew scripture, and continued to focus on Jesus for the meaning of an abundant life.

Chapter Thirteen
When the Dancing Stops

Church attendance is declining in the churches of the United States. The so called "nones" (people with no church affiliation) are quickly arising in number. Churches in the South, the Bible Belt, are so different than just a few generations ago. There was a social expectation about going to church. Most went to church three times each week. There was no skipping a Sunday. There was no sleeping in, or sleeping in church. Church was a barometer of spiritual health. Today the increased mobility keeps people too busy going on the roads to other places. I recall a member of our congregation in Bristol saying about the construction of new paved roads. "When they get those pave roads finished, we'll have overwhelming crowds in the churches." Trouble was that those paved roads. made it more convenient to travel to other places.

The best show in town is no longer the church. Blue laws, youth and family sports activities on Sunday, television, video games, and open stores have captured the eye of people. Today most work on their jobs on weekends. Most people are incredibly inarticulate about faith. No longer do Christians wear twenty-year perfect attendance Sunday School pins. The unbroken circle of the old hymn is now broken. Babies, children, youth, young adults, and older adults are not in attendance. The social concept of adolescence is a recent phenomenon. These people between twelve and twenty keep tradition times for education, a lucrative market for beautiful youth, a relief in the competition for adult jobs, a deterrent to social unrest, an endless source for workers.

Society is now asking whether adolescence is a joyful stage of life. Some people think the fate of joy is bound up fate of beauty, about the experience and visage of youth. Youth is viewed as the golden age when life glistens and humans are open to knowing and sharing joy and wonder. Wonder includes creative energy, romance and solidarity with others. The declining state of our physical appearance brings irritation as smooth skin loses elasticity around the eyes and the chin, and the extra pounds bring sagging in the middle-aged men and women. What a comfort to know that all youthful bodies change. Bodies are separated from the souls at death. The bodies of those who are faithful will be raised and glorified, reunited with the soul, incorruptible for eternity. The resurrected body will be without blemish, powerful and perfect. We will be gorgeous and attractive, full of the joy that God gives. Adolescence is the time we discover our self-identity and our purpose in the world. This stage of youth involves a homeostasis between the inner and outer world.

The possibilities for joy in our youth are almost unlimited. The flowering of puberty brings awareness of the beauty of their young strong bodies. They soon discover the wondrous life beyond family and. church. As a child and now a youth, they enjoy a playful encounter. within a vision quest of happiness. Of course, all ages and all stages of life have unique possibilities for joyful flourishing. The essential nature of adolescents is toward beauty and joy.

So, as we. realize the dance with God has slowed down and even ceased, so the answer is theological. Along with those in and out of the influence of churches has become disenchanted and unable to elicit joy and beauty.

Our youth are subject to drug abuse, consumerism, sexual promiscuity, and a host of emotional and mental problems. Right and wrong are relative and uncommitted sex, cheating, and self-centeredness. Sex offers little more than immediate and carnal meaning. Lacking direction young people are in an aimless drift. Only a healthy theology can show what is beyond mere existence. A Christian life is viewed in our biblical resources as a joyful response to God's glory as demonstrated in the coming of Jesus Christ. Only when spiritual senses are open by contemplating the mystery of Jesus in order that any person can see God's light. And perhaps if the church reclaimed its spirituality, she could redouble the effort to provide the nurture needed to live the possibilities of seeing eyes. and hearing ears to know the true wonder, and beauty, and joy that God provides.

There are no simple solutions to decline. What works in one place may. not work in another. There are no connections between worship style and. renewal, any theological tradition, or contextual cultural practices. We need to reflect as church communities can never soar on autopilot.

Meaningless and joylessness in worship is a symptom of stagnation, and not the direct cause of the decline. Vitality and zeal comes with. theological reflection and choice. Any style is less important than the fact that it has been considered and embraced rather than adopted by. default. Churches that have begun a new dance with God will have a preacher and teacher that connects with the unchurched. If the quality of preaching is high. the people will enjoy it and come back. Successful congregations try different initiatives as experiments. If they work, great, but if not, drop them.

Older people are living longer and healthier. They should be considered. as a prime stage for discipleship. In the future, there will be more seniors than any other age group. There is no simple answer to why the church has been losing the young.

Pastors argued that younger members do not attend church as frequently as older people with the result that, as the older generation dies, attendance. is affected. A more positive way to present this story is that the older generation saw their discipleship as a weekly commitment to worship.

The new emphasis on a joy movement is on parents with young children. Church going is not a priority when Christianity is not a priority. If modern day Christians cannot find one hour to spare, this reflects on the lack of importance they attach to worship. The truth is that the most repeated statement is a lack of belief in the story of Jesus being of saving significance. Those standard complaints concerning competing. commitments and

Sunday attractions sound hollow when set against the. significance of the Christian story. Retaining people of all ages is critical. Enabling a habit to bring children and youth to church is a complete disaster. It is much easier to raise our families as church going people than to turn the unchurched into faithful Christians. Declining and dead churches reflect that gains and losses during adulthood are roughly in balance. The challenge is to. retain the new generation. So "the joy of the Lord" will not be the strength to sustain abundant life for the future. The church as we have known it now has a half-life of one generation. For decade after decade, children have become less spiritual than their parents.

If parents and grandparents identify themselves as belonging to a church while the children do not, why have the born from above people fail to pass it on to their offspring? So, it is no great insight why adolescents increasingly avoid church. The future will not be the same as the past. It is important to understand What is happening. Planning based on false assumptions or wishful thinking is like building a house upon the sand. Obviously, attendance declines as busy people drift away from regular practice. In our day, the young adults find worship to be dull. There is a deepening reservoir of faith to be tapped. The people of God need a new awakening of those who are believing but not belonging. We have thought that people become more religious or spiritual with age. Also, we have assumed that young families will come back after they bring up children, or when one is widowed. However, most of these changes occur for personal reasons not related to having children or. reaching old age. Social forces are not making Americans less religious.

Secularism changes the environment in which children are raised and the chance of effective healthy spiritual upbringing. History has shown that each generation becomes less spiritually minded than the one before.

Declining congregations are unlikely to minister to the community with programs such as food distribution, day care, elderly care, outreach to nursing homes, jails, apartment dwellers, drug abusers, human abuse, debt counseling, shelters, and other projects that meet the needs of people starving for love. Community ministry prepares the ground for conversion, but the links are unclear. Community work increases the. visibility of the church. As Carlyle Marney said," If they must ask where it is, it really doesn't matter if it is." My own theology of joy is in relation to some person, object, or encounter. Joy enhances life when it is shared. So, joy originates. in the mystery of the love shared between God, Jesus, and the Holy Spirit. We could say that they dance together in relations of mutual love. That love is positively full of joy.

Those living with God inside their souls discover this dance of love in worship. It is the kingdom of God.

As a pastor, the baptism of a person who embraces the salvation that Christ offers give me a unique joy as the angels rejoice over one repentant sinner. Usually smiles abound as a new believer receives and gives a testimony of what has happened to them. The new creature in Christ receives God's love and is invited to step lively into the joyous dance of those who now belong to the kingdom where God reigns. By leaning into God's love for us, our souls receive a supernatural boost of joy that reverberates through our lives, into the lives of others, and into eternity.

If we add to our prayer lists all the people we meet in the living of our days, who knows what a difference we may make in their lives? Perhaps as we finally enter heaven, a huge crowd of people who were touched by God's grace through some simple act of kindness, a gift, and our faithful prayers, will be waiting to welcome us home with sheer joy.

Some people retire and rest awhile. Others retire to reinvent themselves. It can be a time of adventure and joyous exploration. Sometimes it is a time of confusion, a time of rejection, or just not feeling wanted. We must accept changing cherished plans as an adult child needs a place to live, hurt in our faith community, a grandchild who needs day care, illness, or an ageing parent whose health issues cause us to be housebound too.

Life is brief and each day we get closer to the presence of God. If we are humble and honest, and curious to know the ways of God, our lives continue that heavenly vision quest to soak up love with each passing year.

Psalm 90:12 says, "Teach us to number our days that we may get a heart of wisdom." We will gain as we reflect on.

how and when and where God has been close to us on our earthly journey. We have used free will to make choices. God has stepped in, time after time, to create blessings out of our mistakes and to enable our good works to bear fruit. A theology of joy causes us to see that we are temples of the Holy Spirit, a unity of body and soul. One day we shall be glorified, cleansed, and. transformed for all eternity.

Perhaps we have stepped upon Jesus' toes during our dance. The music stops. The dance ceases for a little while. Despite our setbacks and current declines, God will continue to ask us to dance in love and joy for the rest of our lives.

Chapter Fourteen
Will You Join in the New Dance?

When I was about ten years old, young enough to be free of teenage anxiety, I had already begun to question the behavior of some adults at church. On this hot summer Sunday, I was grateful that we sung "I Danced in the Morning.". It was a new, upbeat song. We had heard it at Ridgecrest Baptist Conference Center. So, all the kids. knew it and enjoyed it.

In those days, not everybody wanted to sing but about twenty hymns from the church hymnal. When a deacon and his wife heard the first words, they got up and left the worship and huffed out the front doors of the sanctuary. Like most boys, my brother and I asked our parents, "What happened?" They just said, "They didn't like the new song. It was about dancing. Remember the preacher has preached against dancing, smoking, card playing, and things like that."

We did not talk about it then. But several years later, as high school students, we talked about dancing, about joy, and celebrations and why theologically, dancing did not go against the Old Testament or even the New. Testament. The church had told us to read the Bible to find answers. We read where David and the whole house of Israel sang and danced and. played instruments like harps, tambourines, lyres, castanets, and cymbals.

With other boys from other churches, we studied the Psalms in Royal Ambassador camp. We studied psalms of song, music, and dance. Most members of our church had never danced, including me. Later, at the senior prom, my date said she would not go with me if I refused to dance. So, I learned some moves, and I enjoyed it. My pretty date was a member of a so. labeled "more open" church. She said her youth group even held dances in the church basement. We talked about how joy and dancing were no longer proper Christian responses. I told her that I was going to a Baptist college where dancing was not allowed. She shared that dancing was for her an expression of joy and beauty and freedom and that she could not. imagine life without it. "Jim, how can you express the joy of the Lord without dancing?"

Perhaps the church is declining in our day, because it has forgotten what it means to be the people of God. Too many in every generation. have experienced the church as joyless. We have not found the freedom that comes from celebration, empty lives, and no dancing physically or. spiritually. At the end of the Gospel of Luke, Jesus takes his disciples to Bethany where he lifts his hands, blesses them, and ascends to heaven.

After Jesus had gone, the disciples joyfully worshiped in Jerusalem "with great. joy.". They probably entered Jerusalem clapping, singing, and dancing. Joyfully, the disciples witnessed to the world the gift of life that was theirs by the grace of God in Christ Jesus. They had learned a new dance with God and they expressed thanks, awe, compassion, and times of joy.

Joy is an emotion rarely studied in psychology. That is changing. In my own studies and integration of joy into a holistic structure that. enables the articulation of joy as a lived experience. While conducting retreats or Vision quests for Joy as a part of today's joy movement has involved asking people about their own joy experiences. A time of joy is remembered. Using my coaching style, I enable participants to tell. powerfully abundant stories in concrete, experiential details.

Although Christmas can bring depression, grief, and painful memories, the Christmas season is a time for joy. Most recall waking up and swiftly discovering the Christmas tree with many colorfully wrapped gifts. This joy is an elation geyser resulting in jumping up and down, dancing, and expectations fulfilled. I was quite moved by the thousands of stories of overwhelming joy. Sometimes I weep. With humility and appreciation of each person's narrative, I had the feeling of a powerful world full of benevolent persona. Many were so full of gratitude for my time of stimulation of a long-. forgotten, yet life nourishing joy that added to their happiness. They felt safe, good, centered, with a profound sense of being present in the. moment. Each was open to share possible experiences that shared my spirituality and psychology of joy. There was no expected outcome as each shared their journey of joy. Joy emerged as they shared an. encounter in and with their world. Whether they accepted my thoughts or disagreed, joy narratives emerged spontaneously.

Each person's feeling of joy was overwhelmingly intense, powerful, and connected. Affirmed and nurtured, they were full of awe. They were now thankful for the gift of their earthly journey. Abraham Maslow observed that emotions such as joy were peak experiences. Some words that describe his perception include goodness, wholeness, perfection, completion, justice, richness, aliveness, truth, effortlessness, playfulness, and uniqueness.

There have been few studies on the emotion joy, there has been ever fewer. studies of awe. The University of California, Berkeley also received a. Templeton grant for Project Awe, a three-year study. My wife Laurel and I were discussing whether a beautiful Nebraska sunset was a joy or an awe. She said if it was a uniquely colored sunset, it might be a joy, but to her each one is awe. Awe might be a hike through Bryce Canyon, gazing at the Milky Way, or some lovely architecture. Awe is part of our dance with God. Awe binds us together. Each Human is wired with awe. We see things in new ways. Albert Einstein said, "Awe is the source of all true art and science.". Backpacking, camping, white-water rafting, looking at the stars, enjoying amazing music, visiting museums, watching a sunrise are ways church groups in the future might find awe. Gratitude is the heart of church ritual in Holy Communion in the giving and remembering the body and blood of Christ. The experience of gratitude causes us to attribute responsibility to an external agent, to whom we feel grateful whether it is a deity or a person. A person can be grateful for existence, higher powers, or fate. From joy and awe, there forms a flow of gratitude.

Being grateful, people try to enhance goodness in our earthly journey by being compassionate. During my undergraduate years, Douglas Harris introduced me to the work of Martin Buber. Compassion is essential in understanding his "I-Thou" encounter with others. There is no "I" if not related to others. The other, the "Thou," is a tool for our own personal well-being.

The "I-Thou" encounter occurs in a moment of. grace, a gift for which I am thankful. We can reverse the decline of the Christian movement if we sharpen what Buber called "the dialogical. relations. The dialogical life includes cultivation of the community, responsibility, and a life filled with joys. So, the church can learn from Buber, the life with joy and the life with compassion are necessary for "I-Thou," an encounter full of grace and gratitude. The cultivation of the. sacred requires full presence in the world.

That presence is exemplified by. awe and joy. As our vision for my faith community was" to create an atmosphere where joy and miracles happen," that brought in outsiders upon the exchange of compassionate action. Sharing the "joy of the lord" is a key to the decline and death of our congregations. With the "other worldly" stuff that pastors share, there are few places where a person can find happiness and times of joy. I have heard too many preachers give people three easy ways to grasp the meaning and experience of joy in your life.

What I call the "joy movement" is only "a" theology of joy, not "the" theology of joy. Joy is a spiritual gift and a human emotion. The joy from the Spirit is a transformation. This is where joy begins for me. Joy is a moment, a birth, a spark, a seed, a hope, a dream, a glance, a glimmer. Joy comes upon us like little cat feet, a surprise. God has. called the Church to be one. Jesus has prayed that we might be one. Joy comes when we are humbly and honestly working and living and breathing in that one love toward the oneness of the Holy Spirit.

Joy is that experience when you have reached into the depths of your soul and found your unique path where love is the basics of. all your thoughts and actions. Joy reminds us that even when things don't work out, you have done what you can out of love. Love is the foundation of any "joy movement.".

This is not a movement toward one thought or one opinion or political or church. authority's position. That is not our calling as we attempt to renew the. church. I pray that my words provoke a dancing with God with new sorts of dances. My theology of joy is God's plea that we might keep moving, keep thinking, keep reaching out, keep on compassionately doing what the Church has the power to do. By anointing me as the Minister of Joy to. the World, I believe Norman Vincent Peale would say that you can talk about love all you want. If Christianity and churches survive, there must be actions not just talk.

95

With the kingdom of God here and now and with Christ living inside of us, we must begin to reach out, to do, to plan, to discover, and. pray, there will be sheer joy.

Chapter Fifteen
Dancing Gracefully Together

Most of us know instinctively that family should be a source of happiness and times of joy. When the Pittsburgh Pirates won the World Series, the theme song was "We Are Family." Many of the churches where I have been honored to share Vision quests for Joy have been called. family churches. Most were small because they did not define family so that family would include every person who lives in the church's local mission field.

There all kinds of "family." Most do not fit the images of happy couples on a beach laughing together around a meal. Marriage jokes are one thing that exposes the realities from the ideals. Family can be a source of encouragement and joy. Most people have known the deep hurt resulting from parents or relatives. Joylessness in our world is the root of division and separation of. people. Unhappy people not only separate us from one another, but they also separate us from the love of God. Without God that can dam up the flow that must go through those with Christ inside to everyone around us. We seek to get our needs met through all sorts of communities that. lure people into places that make us feel better about ourselves.

To be kingdom of God people, we must let go of allowing our insecurities to be the first thing that walks into a room. Let the love of God in you be that first thing.

The joy movement can help in the need to be loved, accepted, and belong. Part of the human nature of every person is to be flawed. We all have limitations and in our life struggles. We try to dance gracefully with God and others. Kingdom people accept their imperfect reality, their mistakes and weaknesses with vulnerable honesty and humility. Understanding and humility enable us to drop our deceit and selfishness to accept and love ourselves and to "enjoy God forever." This can best be done in a community of strugglers. In a community, we can change, repent, and try fresh again and again and still again, giving dignity to our failures. People do get better at living if we humble ourselves and learn. In their moments of joy, their outside ambitious desires come into a balance with our inner aspiration to become whole.

Joy never can be produced by our own efforts to receive the praises of others. It is best to receive any praise as a surprise, never forced. Joy is a gift that arrives when we least expect it. During those. fleeting moments which you'll never forget, you relish in who you are. and why God sent you to be dancing together with God and his created fellows.

During that awesome time, you shall be satisfied, at peace, at one, as we live together in God's eternal grace. The Bible gives indications that joys and happiness are bound together in relationships. Joy can happen in the grandparent and grandchild (Proverbs 17:6,) husband and wife (Proverbs 5:18, 31, Isaiah 62:5,) parent and child (Proverbs 23:15-16, 24-25, 29:3.) Some women want to be together with a husband. (Genesis 3:16) Most men need a wife. (Genesis 2:18).

Children need parents. Healthy relationships are needed to build healthy families. Being intimately together will not meet all our needs. The dearest and most connected relative cannot provide purpose to your life.

These sorts of expectations will give only disappointment and joylessness. Together we are on a vision quest to seek God. Limited or no interest in God limits joy and satisfaction in any relationship. Family groups create an atmosphere for joy when they fulfill the greater purpose of togetherness with God. Happiness and treasured moments of joy comes from our attitude. toward God. No human can fill the role of God in our life. Without the. awareness of the love of God, the relationships will others will lead to disappointment and failure. Nobody ever replaces God. Dancing through. life together with false expectations will cause us to be frustrated with these. unreasonable demands. Unreal expectations lead to anger and the temptation to quit. We are all stumbles struggling against weaknesses that when redeemed can enable a mysterious strength. In Jeremiah, we find three foundations for a happy life: Hope in a perfect God. (Jer. 9:23-24) Trust in a perfect Word of God. (Jer. 15:16) and the call of God on his life. (Jer.20: 9, 11) As some of my ministry friends would say, "That will preach."

Joy is a spiritual gift from God. Our togetherness gives. additional blessings and a major source for strength and joy. Togetherness brings vulnerability as we share our sins and trust another to share your whole self without another using it to assert her strength. That is what love means. The more you love, the more you can love. Love expands with use.

My wife Laurel and I enjoy watching the reality show "Dancing with the Stars." So, full of beauty with excellent choreography and the incredible moves of the dancing team. The contestants for the dance with grace and a sense of freedom. We enjoy seeing the stars dancing with the professionals. The reaction of the audience and the judges use exaggerated gestures, language, and superlatives. These performances. are extraordinary.

Sometimes the show reveals practices before the show. These clips reveal how they learn to dance with the lovely professionals. Some start with no dancing skills at all. The "stars" are celebrities, sports legends, and other well-known persons. Some collapse, bruise tendons, break bones, or even just quit. The training is constant, enduring, persistent, slow, painstaking, and basic. This learning leads to amazing results. All of us learn to not give up on each other, how to get in synch, dancing together, which sometimes means changing the moves that we already. know. You might even say," If I only had a better partner. The problem. is not with your partner, but both learning to dance together. Walk together and talk to each other. Life is a dance. Enjoy each other as you communicate deeply about big decisions, critical issues and the small trivial experiences of everyday life. An old Chinese proverb says, "If you just walk to go fast, then walk alone, but if you want to go far, walk together."

A word study of joy in the Bible gives answers concerning living together in emotional health and wellbeing. Each time I do this, I understand that joy arises from our attitude toward God as the ultimate source of joy. Scripture says that our joyful moments increase when we. avoid sin and obtaining forgiveness after we sin.

These Bible verses teach that joy comes from some of our own actions. Spiritual discipline and habits are musts for spiritual maturity. Another profitable exercise is to study the Hebrew or Greek words for "happiness.". These words are often translated as "blessing." so my Hebrew professor, Dr. Kenneth Wolfe, advised me to make such a study for my class project as these words tend to be overlooked. Forty-five occurrences of the word "asher" in the Hebrew Scriptures give us some insight about how we can be happy. The Hebrew words are defined more about satisfaction or contentment rather than an emotion, or thrills, or fun or pleasure. The psalm writer of Psalm 1:1-2 and Psalm 40:4 teach that those who refuse ungodly counsel, but instead delight in God's Word will be blessed or happy.

Dancing together in God's love promotes an atmosphere for joy happiness, but without this awareness, people treat affective relationships as they do material objects and the environment. Everything is disposable. So, people use and throw away, take and break, exploit and squeeze to the last drop. Today's me-centered generation causes people to be incapable of looking beyond themselves, and their own needs and wants. People who use others end up being used, manipulated, and discarded by the. same kind of thinking. Even older adults seek independence and now reject. the ideal of growing older together, supporting and looking out for one. another. Contemporary culture suffers from loneliness, coming out of the absence. of God in life and the fragility of our relationships. Older persons are. regarded as a burden. Our current economic problems keep people from participating in life together. With so few possibilities, job offers are. extremely selective and insecure. The phenomenon of street children is getting bigger each day. Sexual slavery and abuse of these children, is too often the result of a child born outside a marriage or family group.

Despite these horrors, the joy of the Lord remains our strength. With the love of Christ whose kingdom is within us, together we share plans, trials, expectations, and concerns. We care for one another and offer mutual forgiveness. Only in this love can we celebrate moments of joy and support each other in the difficult passages of life together. Our communities of faith must include all people from toddlers to seniors. That kind of community will be unique and irreplaceable, both for. our churches and for all the peoples of the earth. Here the joy of love must be carefully cultivated. When our search for pleasure becomes. obsessive, it holds us in thrall and keeps us from experiencing joy. Our joy moments increase pleasure, especially at those times in life when physical pleasure is limited. Our lives are a mixture of enjoyment and. struggles, tensions and rest, satisfactions and longings, but always on a path together to care for each other. Loving another human being includes the joy of contemplating and appreciating their innate beauty. We seek their flourishing even when they. cannot belong to any other. Sometimes this involves when a person is no longer physically appealing but they become intrusive and annoying. Only with the love of God can we open our eyes and see the unique worth of a human creature. My personal theology of joy includes enabling joy in others. This joy is a foretaste of heaven. This fruit of the Spirit is not that of the vain or self-centered, but the experience of lovers who delight in the good of whom they love, who give freely to them bearing fruit. I have through the years collected thousands of personal stories of. moments of joy. Few of these stories are as deep and thrilling as those experienced by two people who love one another. As Mark Twain once said, "On with the dance, let joy be unconfined."

About the Author

The Rev. Dr. James McReynolds is founder of Visionquests for Joy International. He provides spiritual encounters in local churches, hospitals, colleges and schools of higher education, prisons, businesses, and civic organizations.

Norman Vincent Peale declared, "Your preaching embraced with joy, will be, as my positive thinking, a fresh vision for communicating Christian faith. Jim, I anoint you minister of joy to the world."

He has preached in virtually every nation and territory in the world. Millions have read his books, articles, printed sermons, and newsletters. Others have listened to his sermons on radio and television presentations. He is a licensed mental health practitioner and a spiritual director and life clergy coach in Nebraska.

His ecumenical ministry has included service as a public relations specialist for the Sunday School Board of the Southern Baptist Convention, diplomat of the World Pastoral Care Center, the pastoral care committee of the Baptist World Alliance, American Association of Pastoral Counselors, International Positive Psychology Association, prayer and spiritual formation task force of the Cooperative Baptist Fellowship, Radio and Television Commission of the Southern Baptist Convention, United Methodist Mental Health Network, Presbyterian Serious Mental Health Network, state board of directors of the

Mental Health Association of Nebraska, and moderator of the Christian Church (Disciples of Christ) in Nebraska. He serves as regional representative for Global Ministries of the Christian Church (Disciples of Christ) and the United Church of Christ.

His ministry to students has included more than 3,082 campuses throughout the world. He is a frequent speaker for national conventions and conferences.

Licensed in 1954, Jim was ordained in 1960 as a Southern Baptist minister. He also was ordained by Bishop Clay Lee as an elder of the Holston Conference of the United Methodist Church. He now has standing as an ordained minister of the Christian Church (Disciples of Christ.)

His education includes B.A., *magna cum laude*, Carson-Newman University, Jefferson City, Tennessee; graduate assistant in psychology of religion, Baylor University, Waco, Texas; B. J., University of Missouri-Columbia; M.R.Ed., Midwestern Baptist Theological Seminary, Kansas City, Missouri; Th. D., Luther Rice University Theological Seminary, Atlanta, Georgia; Litt.D., Cardiff Theological College, London; M.Div. and D.Min., Vanderbilt University Divinity School, Nashville, Tennessee; Ph.D., California Coast University, Santa Ana; and Psy.D., Graduate Theological Foundation, South Bend, Indiana (Notre Dame, Oxford, and Rome Universities.) He also has had prolific continuing educational experiences to maintain excellence in ministry and licensure as a psychotherapist.

Studies include Princeton Theological Seminary, Lexington Theological Seminary in Kentucky, Candler School of Theology at Emory University in Georgia, clinical pastoral education in various settings, Gottingen University in Germany, Vanderbilt University, Schools of Practical Christianity at Peale Center in New York and Pennsylvania, Integrative Group Psychotherapy Training Institute in Atlanta, Samford University in Birmingham, Yale University Summer Ministry Institute, Presbyterian Theological Seminary at Hastings College, Duke University, Texas Medical Center in Houston, Cotner College Educational Programs in Nebraska, University of Edinburgh in Scotland, University of Virginia, Union Theological Seminary in Virginia, Lake Junaluska Conference Center in North Carolina, Ridgecrest Baptist Conference Center in North Carolina, Glorieta Baptist Conference Center in New Mexico, Montreat Conference Center in North Carolina, Christmount Christian Conference and Retreat Center in North Carolina, Association for Marriage and Family Therapy in Virginia, Furman University in South Carolina, College of William and Mary in Virginia, Holy Land Study Tour, Iliff School of Theology in Colorado, National Association of United Methodist Evangelists annual meetings, American Association of Christian Counselors conventions, Saint Petersburg Theological Academy and Seminary in Russia, Charles University in Prague, World Methodist Conference in Brazil, Pastoral Excellence Program at Emory University in Atlanta, International Congress on Preaching, Episcopal Divinity School Summer Conference and Harvard University Medical School in Massachusetts, Columbia Theological Seminary in Georgia, World Council of Churches meeting in Brazil, Emmanuel School of Religion in

Tennessee, Simpsonwood Retreat Center in Atlanta, Baylor School of Medicine in Dallas, Perkins School of Theology of Southern Methodist University, Mediterranean World in the Time of Saint Paul Vanderbilt Alumni Cruise, Carl Jung Institute in Zurich, Claremont School of Theology in California, Pittsburgh Theological Seminary Leadership Conferences, United States and Mental Health Psychiatric Conference in San Diego, Positive Psychology Center at the University of Pennsylvania in Philadelphia, General Assemblies of the Christian Church (Disciples of Christ) Workshops and Celebrations, Two Rivers Psychiatric Hospital in Kansas City, Virginia Theological Seminary in Alexandria, Mennonite National Mental Health Conferences in North Carolina-Pittsburgh-Norfolk-SanAntonio-Louisville, Spiritual Directors International Annual Conferences, Refresh: National United Methodist Campus Ministers Conferences in Texas and Kansas, Emmaus Road Discipleship School Symposium on the Holy Spirit, and the Word of Life Church Faith and Culture Training with Brian Zahnd and Walter Brueggemann in Saint Joseph, and in 2016-2019 research and project consultant with Yale University Divinity School in New Haven with studies in "Theology of Joy and the Good Life," Clergy Coaching for Change and Resilient Leadership at Bon Secours Retreat and Conference Center in Maryland.

He has been awarded twenty gold-silver-bronze medals for excellence in evangelism in the United Methodist Church, six excellence in evangelism awards in the Christian Church (Disciples of Christ) in the United States and Canada, the Billy Graham Award for Excellence in Evangelism by World Evangelism Federation in New York, and World Missionary

Distinction Award by the Council for World Mission in London, and the governor's honorary award as an Admiral in the Great Navy of the State of Nebraska.

The Christian Church (Disciples of Christ) in Nebraska honored him at the regional board meeting with a plaque reading: "Minister of Joy to the World for his faithful and dedicated service, 2010-2015. We thank him for his high-quality leadership."

www.ingramcontent.com/pod-product-compliance
Lightning Source LLC
Chambersburg PA
CBHW071448030726

47593CB00003B/945